Editor:
  Michael A. Baughen
  assisted by Richard T. Bewes
Music Editor:
  David G. Wilson

Book 2

CONTENTS

INTRODUCTION AND ACKNOWLEDGEMENTS

THE EDITORS determined not to produce a second volume after *Youth Praise 1* unless it was clear that the Lord's hand was upon the preliminary exploration work for such a volume. As they looked at the hundreds of songs available, they found themselves enthusing over so many of them that they were left in no doubt that they should go ahead.

The vast majority of the contents of *Youth Praise 2* has never before been published, and none of it is to be found in our earlier book. There is a variation of style and quality similar to that of *Youth Praise 1*, to cater for the many different types of Youth groups that will use the book. It is the Editors' hope that groups will 'explore' the book thoroughly and not limit themselves to a small selection for regular use. There is much to 'find' here!

The way in which *Youth Praise 1* has been used has been beyond our wildest imaginations and we thank God for this. We 'launch' *Youth Praise 2* with the hope that it may be as much used as *Youth Praise 1* in giving expression to that 'new song' which is in the heart of every believer.

WE ACKNOWLEDGE with gratitude the help we have received from many people in the production of *Youth Praise 2*.

Our publishers have given every possible assistance and we owe much to the Rev. T. Dudley-Smith, the Rev. G. H. Reid and Miss J. Hewitt for all their interest, encouragement and labour and especially to Miss G. Woodward who has handled all the copyright and production details; also to Mrs R. V. Bazire for proof-reading the music; to Mrs A. Corbishley for much secretarial assistance; and to Mrs M. A. Baughen for help in many ways.

In the work of musical arrangement we particularly wish to thank the Rev. N. L. Warren, Mr M. C. T. Strover, Mr G. R. Timms, Mr J. D. Thornton and Rev. O. J. Thomas. As with *Youth Praise 1* this book would not have been possible without the expert technical assistance of the Arnold Reproduction Company and encouragement from Mr F. W. Birkenshaw.

All items in this book are copyright, and the Editors and publishers gratefully acknowledge many kindnesses in permitting the inclusion of copyright material. Every effort has been made to trace copyright-holders, but any errors or omissions will **gladly** be put right at the first opportunity.

M. A. B.
D. G. W.
R. T. B.

For a complete list of Falcon books and booklets and CPAS audio-visual aids write to:

CPAS PUBLICATIONS
Falcon Court, 32 Fleet Street, London EC4Y 1DB

Praise

151 Let us praise

Words and Music: **G. Brattle**

Let us praise, as we raise heart and voice to God a-bove

Let it ring, As we sing out the sto - ry of His love.

Let it flow, Let it grow, Let it rise from ev-'ry shore: Be ad-

-ored, Christ the Lord, Praise His Name for ev - er - more!

152 Let us praise God together

Words: J.E. Seddon
Music: Calhoun Melody
arr. D.G. Wilson

2. Let us seek God together,
   Let us pray,
   Let us seek His forgiveness
   As we pray.
      He will cleanse us from all sin,
      He will help us the fight to win,
      His Name be exalted on high.

3. Let us serve God together,
   Let us serve;
   Let our lives show His goodness
   As we work.
      Christ the Lord is the world's true light,
      Let us serve Him with all our might;
      His Name be exalted on high.

153 Blessed be the Lord

Words: Psalm 68.19
Music: John van den Hogen

Bless-ed be the Lord____ who dai- ly bears us up,____

E   G#7 C# C#7   F#m

__ He takes our cares.____ Blessed be the Lord.____

B7   E

__ Ev - en the God___ ___ of our sal - va - tion. __

B+   Bm   C#   F#m

__ Blessed be the Lord.   Blessed be the Lord.____

B7   E

© John van den Hogen 1969. By kind permission.

154 I've got something to sing about

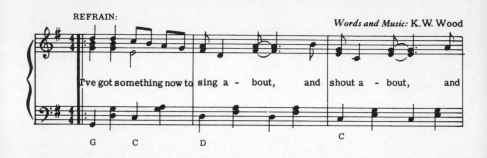

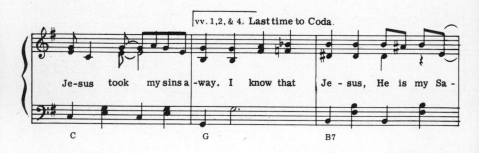

poured on Him my Lord and He did it for me,___ so that I could be free

A7   D   D7

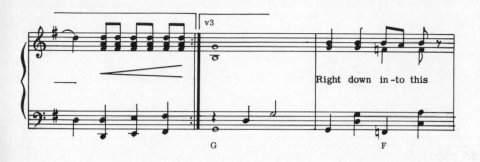

v3

Right down in-to this

G   F

sin - sick world,___ from heav - en's glo - ry He came

E   Am   G   F

To bleed and die on Cal - va-ry's cross to

E   Am   G   C   F

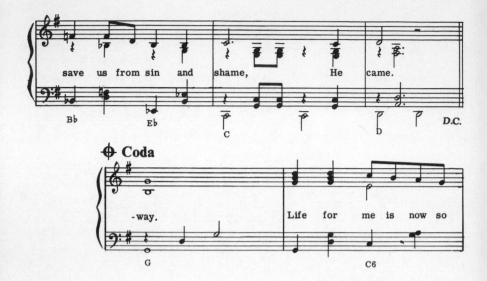

save us from sin and shame, He came.

Bb   Eb   C   D   D.C.

⊕ **Coda**

-way.   Life for me is now so

G   C6

won - der - ful, since Je - sus took my sins a - way.

D   C   G

2. I've got something now to sing about, and shout about, and tell around.
Life for me is now so wonderful, since Jesus took my sins away.
Each day now ev'rywhere that I go I know Jesus is there by my side.
His life within helps me to win over anger and pride, 'cos He's living inside.

3. I've got ev'rything to sing about, and shout about, and tell around.
Oh just let me tell to ev'ryone, how Jesus died and rose again.
Right down into this sin-sick world, from heaven's glory He came.
To bleed and die on Calvary's cross to save us from sin and shame, He came.

4. I've got ev'rything to sing about, and shout about, and tell around.
Oh just let me tell to ev'ryone, how Jesus died and rose again.
Each day now ev'rywhere that I go I know Jesus is there by my side.
His life within helps me to win over anger and pride, 'cos He's living inside.

I've got ev'rything to sing about, and shout about, and tell around.
Life for me is now so wonderful, since Jesus took my sins away.
Life for me is now so wonderful, since Jesus took my sins away.

155 There is joy

Words and Music: M.J.H. Fox

There is joy, there is joy, There is joy be-fore the an-gels ov - er

E   Emaj.7   E6   E

Ev - 'ry per -son who re -pents of sin. There is joy, there is

B7   E   A   E

joy There is joy be-fore the an-gels ov - er Ev - 'ry

E maj.7   E6   E   B7

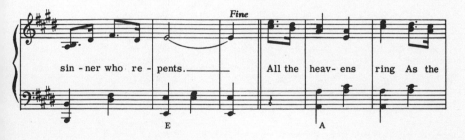

Fine

sin - ner who re - pents.____ All the heav - ens ring As the

E   A

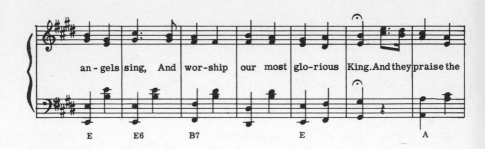

an-gels sing, And wor-ship our most glo-rious King. And they praise the

E   E6   B7   E   A

name Of the Lord who came To seek the blind and lost and lame.

E   E6   F#7   B7

© M.J.H. Fox 1969. By kind permission.

156 Lord of the years

Words: T. Dudley-Smith
Music: M.A. Baughen and D.G. Wilson

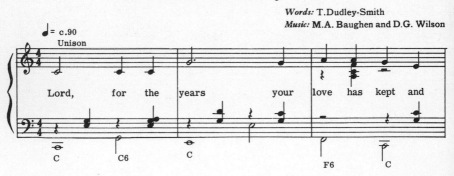

♩ = c.90
Unison

Lord,   for   the   years   your   love   has   kept   and

C   C6   C   F6   C

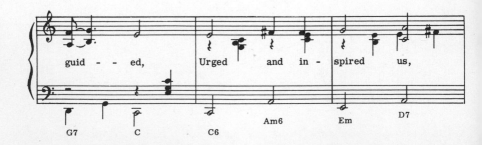

guid - - ed,   Urged   and in - spired   us,

G7   C   C6   Am6   Em   D7

cheered us on___ our way, Sought___ us and

G   Am7   D7   G   C

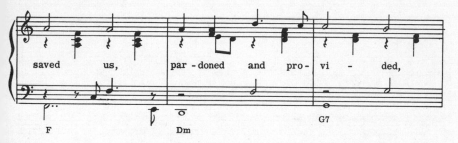

saved   us,   par - doned   and   pro - vi - ded,

F   Dm   G7

Lord   of the   years,   we   bring our thanks   to- day.

Am   Em   C   F   Dm   G7   C

2. Lord, for that Word, the Word of life which fires us,
    Speaks to our hearts and sets our souls ablaze.
    Teaches and trains, rebukes us and inspires us,
    Lord of the Word, receive your people's praise.

3. Lord, for our land, in this our generation,
    Spirits oppressed by pleasure, wealth and care;
    For young and old, for commonwealth and nation,
    Lord of our land, be pleased to hear our prayer.

4. Lord, for our world, when men disown and doubt Him,
    Loveless in strength and comfortless in pain;
    Hungry and helpless, lost indeed without Him,
    Lord of the world, we pray that Christ may reign.

5. Lord for ourselves; in living power remake us -
    Self on the cross and Christ upon the throne -
    Past put behind us, for the future take us,
    Lord of our lives, to live for Christ alone.

157 Sing praise

Words: Johann Jakob Schultz
tr. Frances Elizabeth Cox
Music: D. Phillips

soul He fills,   And ev-'ry faith-less   murmur stills:

C6   Am   D7   C   F#°   G

To God all praise and   glo - ry.

Em   Am   D7   G   C

Last verse only.

G   C   G   C   G

2. What God's almighty power hath made,
    His gracious mercy keepeth;
    By morning glow or evening shade
    His watchful eye ne'er sleepeth;
    Within the kingdom of His might,
    Lo! all is just and all is right:
    To God all praise and glory.

3. The Lord is never far away,
    But, through all grief distressing,
    An ever-present help and stay,
    Our peace, and joy, and blessing;
    As with a mother's tender hand,
    He leads His own, His chosen band:
    To God all praise and glory.

4. Thus, all my toilsome way along,
    I sing aloud Thy praises,
    That men may hear the grateful song
    My voice unwearied raises;
    By joyful in the Lord, my heart,
    Both soul and body bear your part:
    To God all praise and glory.

158 Be this my joy today

Words and Music: G. Brattle

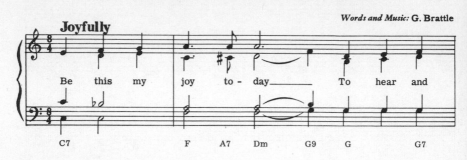

Be this my joy to-day____ To hear and

to ob-ey My Sav-iour's word,____ His won-der-ful

word____ To read in ev-'ry line God's will, and

make it mine____ Be this my joy____ my won-der-ful joy!____

159 In my heart

Words: (Dans Mon Cœur) C. Roda
Trans. M. Ponsford and M.A. Baughen
Music: C. Roda and J. Lacombe

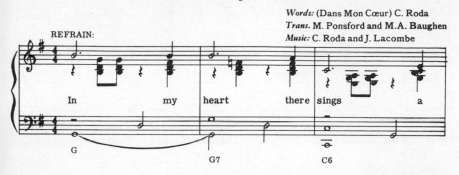

In my heart there sings a

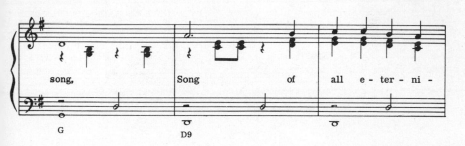

song, Song of all e - ter - ni -

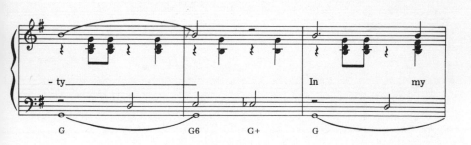

- ty_____ In my

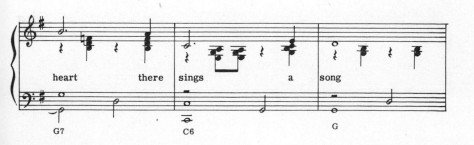

heart there sings a song

To verse

Of my Sa - viour's love to me.

D9   G

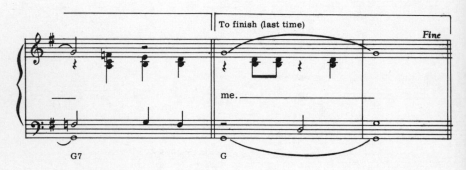

To finish (last time)

Fine

me.

G7   G

VERSES:

He for me left be - hind the Fa - ther's

C6   Em7   Am   D7   G

throne for me, just a sin - ner like

G   Am7   D7

me. _____ And for me He was

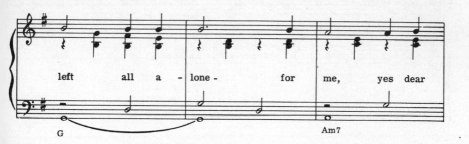

left all a - lone - for me, yes dear

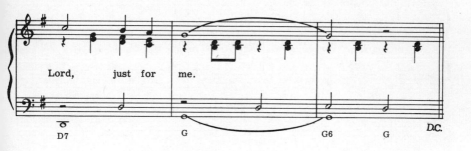

Lord, just for me.

2. He for me came to be crucified -
   For me, just a sinner like me.
   And for me came to suffer and die -
   For me, yes dear Lord, just for me.
   Chorus

3. He for me rose again from the grave -
   For me, just a sinner like me.
   And for me He will come back one day -
   For me, yes dear Lord, just for me.
   Chorus

Psalmody
160 Blessed is the man (Psalm 1)

Words arr: M.A.Baughen
Music: M.A. Baughen
arr: J.D. Thornton

man. But his de - light by day and

F C7 F Gm7 C7 F

For last two lines D.S.al Fine

night Is the law of God Al - migh - ty.

Gm7 C7 F7 Bb Gm F C7 F

2. He is like a tree - a tree that flourishes
   Being planted by the water - blessed is that man.
   He will bring forth fruit - his leaf will wither not -
   For in all he does he prospers - blessed is that man.
   For his delight - by day and night -
   Is the law of God Almighty.

3. The wicked are not so - for they are like the chaff-
   Which the wind blows clean away - the wicked are not so.
   The wicked will not stand - on the judgment day -
   Nor belong to God's people - the wicked will not stand.
   But God knows the way of righteous men
   And ungodly ways will perish.

   Blessed is the man, the man who does not walk
   In the counsel of the wicked - blessed is that man.

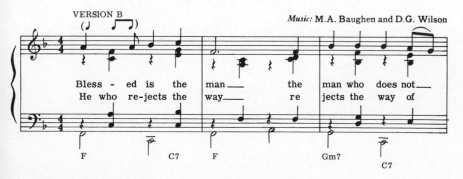

VERSION B

Music: M.A. Baughen and D.G. Wilson

Bless - ed is the man ___ the man who does not ___
He who re-jects the way ___ re jects the way of

F C7 F Gm7 C7

161 Why do the heathen (Psalm 2)

Words arr: M.A.Baughen
Music: M.A. Baughen and J.D. Thornton

Why do the heathen con - spire?

Peoples are plotting in vain, Kings of the earth de -

-clare A - gainst God and His A - nointed One:

Break all their bonds a - sun - der,

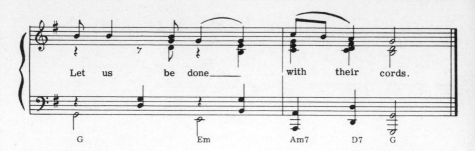

Let us be done____ with their cords.

G   Em   Am7   D7   G

2. He who is sitting in heaven
Laughs them to scorn, as the Lord,
He will address them in wrath
And they fear as they listen to His words:
'I have set up my true King,
He is on my holy hill.'

3. This is the word from the Lord -
He told me, 'You are my son:
Ask of me and I will make
All the nations of earth your heritage.
You shall bruise them with iron
Dash them in pieces like a vase'.

4. Now therefore, kings of the earth,
Think and take warning from this.
Yield to the Lord and serve Him
Kneeling down before Him in reverence.
Do not ignore and perish
Blessed are all those who trust in Him.

© M.A. Baughen and J.D. Thornton 1969. By kind permission.

162 O Lord our God (Psalm 8)

Words and Music: M.A.Baughen
arr: J.D. Thornton

Refrain

O Lord, our God! How ma-jes-tic is your

C7   F   Am   Dm   Gm7

To Coda **(5th time)**
Verse

name in all the earth!   1. Your glo - ry is tran -

C7   F   Bb   C6

-cen - dent Yet chil - dren sing your praise Your

F   Dm   Gm7   F   Bb   C7

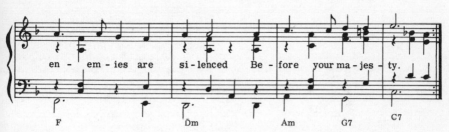

en - em - ies are si - lenced Be - fore your ma - jes - ty.

F   Dm   Am   G7   C7

✛ Coda

O Lord, Our God! How ma-jes-tic is your name in all the earth!

F7 Bb D7   Gm   A7   Dm Gm7 C7   F

2. I stand to view the heavens
   Created by your hands
   You placed the moon and stars there
   And yet you care for man.
      O Lord, our God!
      How majestic is your name in all the earth!

3. To man you gave such honour
   You made him almost god
   In giving him dominion
   Over created things.
      O Lord, our God!
      How majestic is your name in all the earth!

4. You put beneath man's ruling
   All animals of earth
   The birds that fly above him
   And all within the sea.

   O Lord, our God!
   How majestic is your name in all the earth!
   O Lord, our God!
   How majestic is your name in all the earth!

163 O Lord our Lord(Psalm 8)

Words: E. Bash
Music: Traditional
arr. D.G. Wilson

2. When I think on Thy heavens, the work of Thy fingers,
   The moon and the stars which Thou hast ordained
   What is man in Thy mem'ry, a man that Thou mindest
   The son of man that Thou carest for him.

3. Thou hast made him just lower than angels of glory,
   And crowned him with honour and glory and power.
   Thou gavest dominion o'er all of the wide earth,
   And all of the creatures that run in the sea.

164 The Lord is my Shepherd (Psalm 23)

Words: J.E. Seddon
Music: N.L. Warren

1. The Lord is my Shepherd, I nev - er shall want; He

makes me in pas - tures to lie;___ Be - side the still wa - ters He

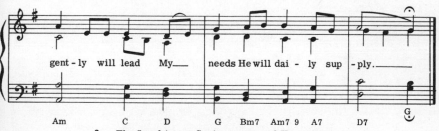

gent - ly will lead My___ needs He will dai - ly sup - ply.___

2. The Lord is my Saviour, my soul He restores,
   He found me when lost and astray;
   He shows me the way of His Truth and His will
   And helps me to trust and obey.

3. The Lord is my shield, I no evil shall fear;
   He lightens the dark paths I tread;
   He always is with me, my rod and my staff,
   And now death itself has no dread.

4. The Lord is my strength, at His table I find
   The pow'r to defeat all my foes;
   My life He sustains with His kindness and power
   With blessing my cup overflows.

5. The Lord is my song, of His grace I will sing,
   I'll dwell in His house all my days;
   His goodness and mercy will follow me still,
   His Name I for ever will praise.

165 The earth is the Lord's (Psalm 24)

Words arr: M.A. Baughen
Music: M.A. Baughen and D.G. Wilson

2.   So who shall ascend on the hill of the Lord?
     Or stand in the holiest place?
     He whose hands are clean and heart is pure
     Who is not false and is not deceitful.

3.   And he will receive all the blessing of God
     His Saviour will vindicate him
     Such is everyone who seeks the Lord
     Who seeks the face of the God of Jacob.

4.   Now lift up your heads O you gates and you doors
     The King of all Glory comes in!
     Who then is this King of Glory - who?
     The Lord Himself who is strong and mighty.

5.   Now lift up your heads O you gates and you doors
     The King of all Glory comes in!
     Who then is this King of Glory - who?
     The Lord of Hosts is the King of Glory!

166 The Lord is my light (Psalm 27)

Words arr: **M.A. Baughen**
Music: A. Plank
arr. D.G. Wilson

The Lord is my light and sal - va - tion in life The Lord is my strong___ hold, so whom shall I fear? Though men may as - -sail me They will stum - ble and fall For though bat - tles rage,___ I will trust in the

1 & 2

Lord! 2.One see all Your good - ness, O Lord!

2. One thing which I seek is to live in God's house
    To gaze on His beauty and learn more of Him
    In trouble He will protect me
    Lifting my head
    And I will rejoice and will sing to the Lord'.

3. O Lord hear my voice when I call upon You,
    You said 'Seek my face' and Your face do I seek.
    In anger do not reject me
    You are my help
    I know I will see all Your goodness, O Lord!

167 I waited patiently (Psalm 40)

Words arr: M.A. Baughen
Music: M.A. Baughen and D.G. Wilson

1. I wait - ed pat -ient-ly for the Lord He turned and

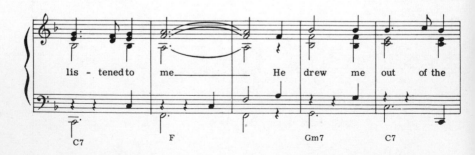

lis - tened to me_____ He drew me out of the

ech - o-ing pit And out of the mi - ry clay. He

set my feet up - on a rock My foot - steps

He made se - cure With - in my mouth He

put a new song A song of praise to God.

2. In many seeing it, fear will come -
They then will turn to the Lord
And he is happy who trusts in the Lord
Who will not be led astray.
Your wondrous deeds and thoughts to us
Are multiplied, O my God -
They number more than we can proclaim
Lord! None compares with You!

3. It is not offerings You require
But open ears to Your word
And so instead of a sacrifice
I come to You with my life.
I love to do Your will, my God,
Within my heart is Your law;
Deliverance is news I have told -
My lips have not been sealed.

4. I have not hidden within my heart
Your steadfast love and Your help -
The congregation has heard me declare
Salvation and faithfulness.
And so when evils circle me
Have mercy on me, O Lord
May all who love You thankfully say:
The Lord is great indeed!

168 Have mercy Lord (Psalm 51)

Words: J.M. Barnes
Music: D.G. Wilson

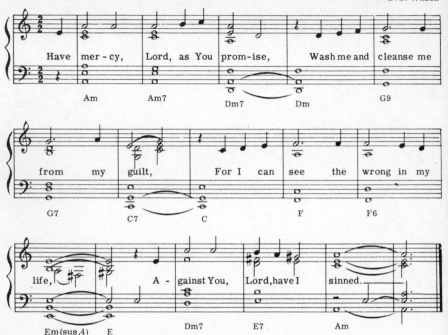

Have mer-cy, Lord, as You prom-ise, Wash me and cleanse me from my guilt, For I can see the wrong in my life, A - gainst You, Lord, have I sinned.

2. In judgment, Your word is blameless,
   For I have sinned since my beginning,
   And Lord, You long for truth in my life,
   So give me wisdom today.

3. Lord, wash me from my uncleanness,
   Fill me with joy where once was sadness,
   Give me a heart renewed, O my Lord,
   A new right spirit within.

4. Turn from my sins and destroy them,
   But let me never be forsaken.
   O give me joy in knowing You save,
   And make me love Your command.

5. I'll tell all those who ignore You
   And sinners then will come repentant.
   Lord, save me from the death I deserve
   Then I will tell what You've done.

6. Lord take my lips and I'll praise You;
   No sacrifice I bring redeems me.
   All that You want is my broken heart;
   A gift You will not refuse.

7. Lord give Your peace to Your servant.
   Protect and stay by me for ever.
   Through Your great love accept what I give
   And fill my life with Your praise.

169 If the building (Psalm 127)

Words and Music: D.G. Wilson

VERSE

If the build-ing is not of the Lord, There's
Lord is not watch-ing the town, There's

no use in start-ing the build-ing. If the
no point in hav-ing it guard-ed.

REFRAIN

Praise Him in whom we can trust

Je-sus our rock, our strong de-fence. Praise

Him for life that's se - cure, For love that

will not end.   2. You're   end.

Bb6   C7   F   Bb   F   C7   F   Bb   F

2. You're careful to wake with the dawn.
   For your wages you toil till the evening.
   But the Lord gives the ones that He loves
   All His gifts even while they are sleeping.
   Chorus

3. Every child is a gift of the Lord,
   Those we love a great joy and a blessing,
   It is great to be blessed of the Lord,
   It's the life with which no-one can quarrel.
   Chorus

© D.G. Wilson 1969. By kind permission.

170 Faithful vigil ended (Nunc Dimittis)

Words: T. Dudley-Smith
Music: D.G. Wilson

1. Faith-ful vi - gil end - ed, Watching, wait- ing cease;
2. All Thy spir-it prom-ised, All the Fa - ther willed,

C   Cmaj.7   C9   C7   F   Bb   F

Mas-ter, grant Thy ser - vant His dis - charge in peace.
Now these eyes be - hold it Per -fect- ly ful - filled.

Dm7   G11   C6   Cmaj.7   F   G7   C

Ped———— *

3. This Thy great deliverance
   Sets Thy people free;
   Christ their light uplifted
   All the nations see.

4. Christ, Thy people's glory!
   Watching, doubting cease;
   Grant to us Thy servants
   Our discharge in peace.

© T. Dudley-Smith and D.G. Wilson 1969. By kind permission.

171 Gloria in Excelsis

Words arr: C. J. Laslett
Music: M.A. Baughen
arr. N.L. Warren

2. Lamb of God in triumph seated,
Jesus Christ our great high priest,
By your all-sufficient offering
You have cancelled all our sins.
  So through you we come with boldness,
  Fearless, to the Father's throne.
  Justified by faith, rejoicing,
  Lord and God we praise your name!

3. Holy Spirit, Lord, proceeding
From the Father and the Son,
You're the seal of our salvation.
Live and reign within our hearts.
  Father, Son and Holy Spirit,
  You alone are God Most High.
  Maker, Saviour, Sanctifier,
  Lord and God we praise your name!

alternative to verse 2

Lamb of God, Messiah, Jesus
God the Father's only Son,
Pity us, have mercy on us
You who take away our sins.
  You remove the world's offences,
  Hear us Lord. Receive our prayer.
  Pity us, have mercy on us,
  You who sits at God's right hand.

God
172 I know

Words and Music: The Crossbeats
arr: J. and B. Courtie

know, I know He's mine for ev-er - more.O yes I

Eb   Fm7   Eb Ab   Eb Ab

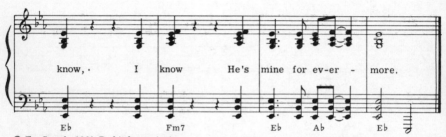

know, · I know He's mine for ev-er - more.

Eb   Fm7   Eb Ab   Eb

173 High over the world

Words and Music: Betty Lou Mills

Rhythmically

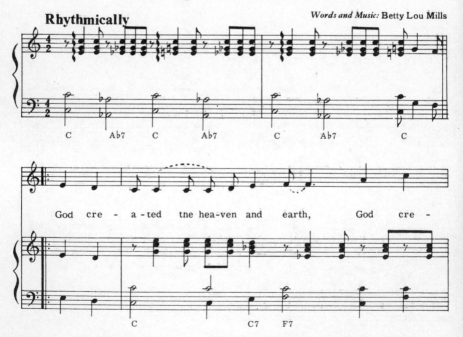

C   Ab7   C   Ab7   C   Ab7   C

God cre - a -ted the hea-ven and earth, God cre -

C   C7 F7

world.

C   Ab7   C   Ab7   C   Ab7   C

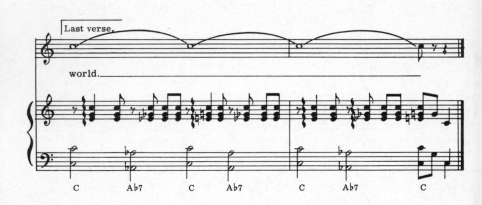

Last verse.

world.

C   Ab7   C   Ab7   C   Ab7   C

2.   God created the seasons,
     God created the stars:
     God created the fish and the fowl
     God created the cattle and beasts -
     He is high ...

3.   God created man and woman
     In His image from the dust:
     And His power is yet the same
     If in Him we'll put our trust -
     He is high...

174 They say He's wonderful

Words: H. Pollock
arr: D. Delarue

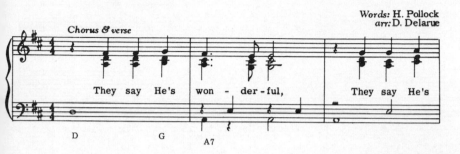

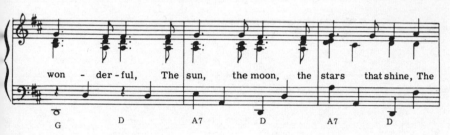

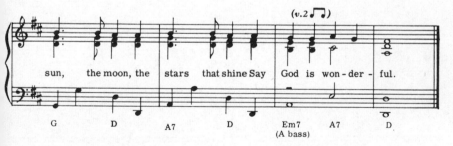

1. He makes the rain to fall
    He sees the wheat grow tall
    The root, the shoot and soon the fruit,
    The root, the shoot and soon the fruit,
    It shows He cares for all.
    Chorus

2. When I see babies small,
    And I hear children call,
    And think of family life and fun,
    And think of family life and fun,
    I know He's behind it all
    Chorus

3. The love men have for Him
    Such love death cannot dim,
    Of small and great of rich and poor,
    Of small and great of rich and poor,
    Love like this comes from Him.
    Chorus

4. And I know He's wonderful,
    I know He's wonderful,
    The Son of God who died for me,
    The Son of God who died for me,
    I know He's wonderful.
    Chorus

175 God is there

Words: A.H. Zoller and F. Rauch
tr. S. Lonsdale and M.A. Baughen
Music: A.H. Zoller

Je -sus   we're   His!_____   God is   And   in

Je - sus   we're   His!_____

2.   Satan offers his own happiness
     And we're tempted to turn from the Lord
     Yet we know that such happiness fades
     Without God we are helpless and poor.
       Chorus

3.   Men make wars in this sin-ridden world
     Men have hearts in which selfishness reigns
     Men so often refuse to forgive
     Yet God loves us in spite of it all.
       Chorus

4.   God was there when the world first began
     He'll be there when it passes away
     Everything is dependent on Him
     God is there just wherever we are
       Chorus

176 I love the flowers

Words and Music: G. McClelland
arr. P. Bye

I love the flowers, I love the trees, most of all I love dai - sies, I love the riv-ers and the moun-tains high, But I don't love as much as God. Be-cause

42

177 Lord you sometimes speak in wonders

Words: C. Idle
Music: N.L. Warren

Lord, you sometimes speak in wonders Un - mis-tak- a - ble and clear;

F Fmaj7 Dm7   Gm   C7   F Fmaj7   Dm7   Gm Gm7 C7

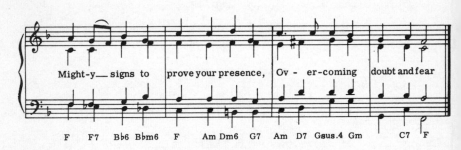

Might-y__ signs to   prove your presence, Ov - er-coming doubt and fear

F   F7   Bb6 Bbm6   F   Am Dm6 G7   Am D7 Gsus.4 Gm   C7 F

2. Lord, you sometimes speak in whispers,
    Still and small and scarcely heard;
    Only those who want to listen
    Catch the all-important word.

3. Lord, you sometimes speak in silence,
    Through our loud and noisy day:
    We can know and trust you better
    When we quietly wait and pray.

4. Lord, you often speak in Scripture -
    Words that summon from the page,
    Shown and taught us by your Spirit
    With fresh light for every age.

5. Lord, you always speak in Jesus,
    Always new yet still the same;
    Teach us now more of our Saviour;
    Make our lives display His Name.

178 Our Father

Words: T. Dudley-Smith
Music: M.A. Baughen
arr. D.G. Wilson

Fa - ther who formed the fa - mi - ly of man,___ High throned in hea - ven ev - er-more the same Our prayer is still as Christian prayer began, That hallowed be your Name. -more.

2. Lord of all Lords, the only King of kings,
Before whose countenance all speech is dumb,
Hear the one song the new creation sings -
Your promised kingdom come!

3. Father of mercy, righteousness and love,
Shown in the sending of that only Son,
We ask on earth, as in the realms above,
Your perfect will be done!

4. Lord of the harvest and the living seed,
The Father's gift from which the world is fed,
To us your children grant for every need
This day our daily bread.

5. Father, whose Son ascended now in heaven
Gave once Himself upon a cross to win
Man's whole salvation, as we have forgiven,
Forgive us all our sin.

6. Lord of all might and majesty and power,
Our true Deliverer and our great Reward,
From every evil, and the tempter's hour,
Deliver us, good Lord.

7. Father who formed the family of man,
Yours is the glory heaven and earth adore,
The kingdom and the power, since time began,
Now and for evermore.

179 If God desires it

Words: E. Vargas
Trans. S. Lonsdale and M.A. Baughen
Music: E. Vargas
arr. A.H. Zoller

If God de-sires it, all the flow'rs on earth will be red, If God de-sires it all the stones will turn in-to bread, If God all-ows it we can play With moon and stars and milk - y way Or

C   C maj.7   Dm   G   Dm7   G9   C maj.7   C   C7   F

And re - live our lives a - gain for

Bb7   Am7

bet - ter or for worse! Yet if we real - ly

G7   C   F

could   Would it be for our good   Much

C9   G7   C6

bet - ter that our ways be - long to

G7   C6

Him who un - der - stands   Much bet - ter that   our

G   C   F7

dest - i - ny   is safe - ly   in   His hands

Em7   G7   C   *D.C. al Fine*

© Gustav Bosse Verlag, Germany, By kind permission.

180 The hills in their beauty

Words and Music: D. Kennedy
arr. D.G. Wilson

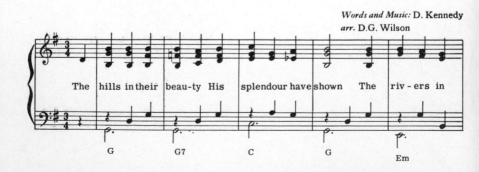

The hills in their beau-ty His splendour have shown The riv - ers in

G   G7   C   G   Em

181 Beyond the grasp

Words: M. Saward
Music: M.A. Baughen and D.G. Wilson

Be - yond the grasp of hu - man brain, Great God, ma - jest - ic Ru - ler, We men by faith, Your pre - sence find In Christ, our ris - en Mas - ter, And___

all the pow'r which we can use Through tur - bine, jet and

G   Em7   Am   D7   G   Am7   G

mo - tor Is___ no - thing to the

A7   D   G   C   Am   D7   Bm

pow'r of ___ Christ Who frees us from dis - as - ter.

Em   Am   D   D7   G   C   Am7   D7   G

2. For we believe, despite the power
    Of greed and lust and Satan
    Which dominates the will of men,
    That sin can be forgiven.
    In humble trust and confidence
    No power our souls can frighten
    We spread your liberating truth
    That speaks of love in heaven.

3. Yet here, within your universe.
    We struggle with the Tempter
    He has no right to trick and trap,
    No right to make us cower.
    So, Spirit of the living Christ,
    The Saviour and the Victor,
    That we may daily overcome
    Uphold us with your power.

182 Who holds the keys?

Words: D. Green (Based on Revelation 1.17-18)
Music: R.T. Bewes
arr. M.C.T. Strover

The fu-ture now is dark, the path un-known; God's peo-ple walk in night and seem a-lone. When will the promised time come, and it all be shown - God in con-trol - God on the throne?

2. Though nations rise and fall and kingdoms sway.
Though wars and tumults rage day after day;
His promise stands though heaven and earth may pass away;
His word remains - true for today.

3. How much we need His Word in hours like these!
More powerful than the threats of enemies:
Above the raging of the storms and mighty seas -
He is the Lord, He holds the keys.

4. Of life and death and hell, and every throne,
He only holds the keys and He alone;
Of heaven and glory and of all eternities,
He is the Lord - He holds the keys.

183 God is all-loving

German Words and Music: A. Rische

God is all_ lov - ing He has re - deemed me,

God is all lov - ing, and He loves me.

Chorus

And so I sing a-gain, God is all_ lov - ing

God is all_ lov - ing, and He loves me.

2. I lay in bondage to sin's dominion
   And as I lay I could not get free.
   Chorus

3. I lay within the death-grip of Satan
   Sin pays its servants wages of death.
   Chorus

4. But He sent Jesus, to be our Saviour
   But He sent Jesus, who set me free.
   Chorus

5. By pledge of pardon He loosed my burden
   His Holy Spirit lifted my load.
   Chorus

6. Your love is patient with my shortcomings
   Your love upholds me in all my need.
   Chorus

7. Your joy refreshes my fainting spirit
   Your peace envelops my troubled heart.
   Chorus

8. Now I inherit eternal riches
   Through You inherit eternal rest.
   Chorus

9. O love eternal, I'll ever praise You
   For ever more Your love I'll proclaim.
   Chorus

Jesus
184 From Bethlehem to Calvary

Words and Music: Charles Roda
Trans. Mike Ponsford (adapted)
arr. John van den Hogan and D.G. Wilson

From Beth - le-hem to Cal - va - ry   From the crib to the

D   D7   G6   G   D

cru - el tree, From des-pair to joy for me,

E7   A7   D   D7   G   D

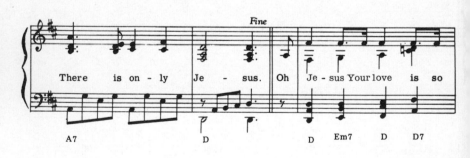

Fine

There is on - ly Je - sus. Oh Je - sus Your love is so

A7   D   D   Em7   D   D7

great to me that it reach-es the depths of my heart.   Oh

G   Am7   G   D   Em7   D   Em7   A7

Je - sus, Your love, all Your love for me, Makes my fear and my sor-row de -

D   Em7   D   D7   G   Am7   G   Bm   E7   A7

-part.   I   want ev - 'ry - one to know

D   G   D

Of   the   one   who loves me   so___   Christ   a- lone   can

Em7   A7   D   D7   G

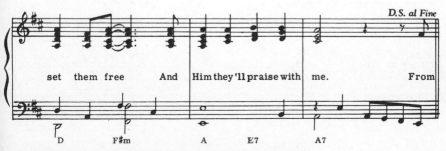

D.S. al Fine

set   them free   And   Him they 'll praise with   me.   From

D   F#m   A   E7   A7

185 Christ is the Lord

Words: K. Preston
Music: D. Brace and D. Baggs

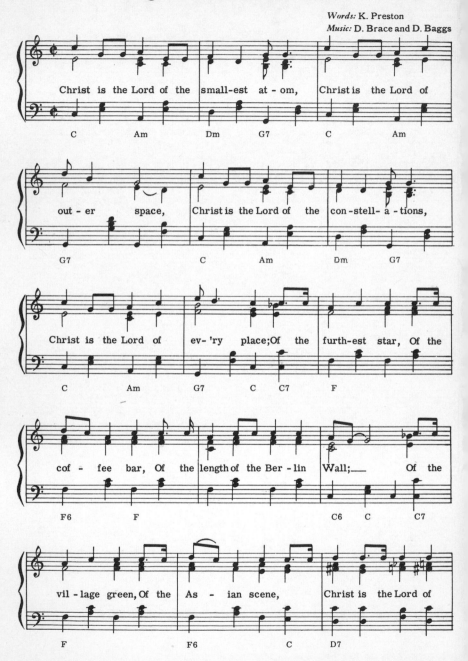

Christ is the Lord of the small-est at - om, Christ is the Lord of out - er space, Christ is the Lord of the con-stell- a -tions, Christ is the Lord of ev- 'ry place; Of the furth-est star, Of the cof - fee bar, Of the length of the Ber - lin Wall;—— Of the vil - lage green, Of the As - ian scene, Christ is the Lord of

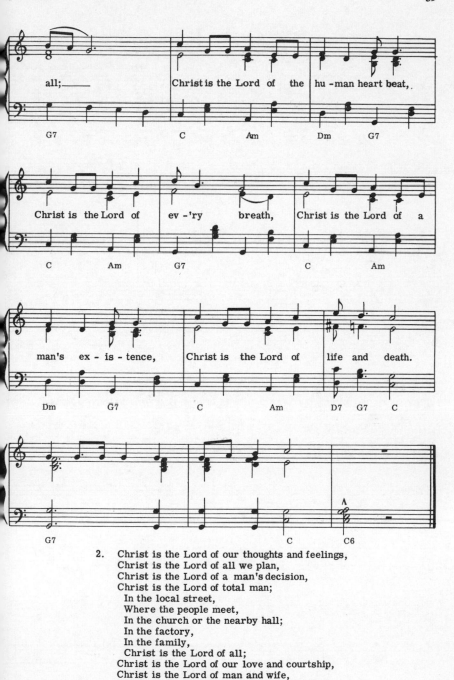

all;____ Christ is the Lord of the hu-man heart beat,

Christ is the Lord of ev-'ry breath, Christ is the Lord of a

man's ex-is-tence, Christ is the Lord of life and death.

2. Christ is the Lord of our thoughts and feelings,
    Christ is the Lord of all we plan,
    Christ is the Lord of a man's decision,
    Christ is the Lord of total man;
        In the local street,
        Where the people meet,
        In the church or the nearby hall;
        In the factory,
        In the family,
        Christ is the Lord of all;
    Christ is the Lord of our love and courtship,
    Christ is the Lord of man and wife,
    Christ is the Lord of the things we care for,
    Christ is the Lord of all our life.

186 Only Jesus

Moderato

Words and Music: Betty Lou Mills

Who took fish and bread hun - gry people fed? Who changed wa - ter in - to wine? Who made well the sick, who made see the blind? Who touched earth with feet di- -vine? On - ly Je - sus, On - ly Je - sus,

2. Who walked dusty road? Cared for young and old?
    Who sat children on His knee?
    Who spoke words so wise? Filled men with surprise,
    Who gave all, but charged no fee?
    Only Jesus, Only Jesus, Only He has done this:
    Who in death and grief spoke peace to a thief?
    Only Jesus did all this.

3. Who soared through the air? Joined His Father there?
    He has you and me in view:
    He, who this has done, is God's only Son,
    And he's int'rested in you.
    Only Jesus, Only Jesus, Only He has done this:
    He can change a heart, give a new fresh start,
    Only He can do this.

187 I've tried in vain

Words: Verses 1 and 2, J. Proctor
Verses 3 and 4, R.J. Mayor
Music: R.J. Mayor

I've tried in vain a thous-and ways My fears to quiet, my hopes to raise: But what I need, the Bi-ble says Is ev-er on-ly Je-sus. He died, He lives, He reigns, He pleads, There's love in all His works and deeds; There's all a guil-ty sin-ner needs For-ev-er-more in Je-sus. For all things work to-

188 Through all our days

Words: M. Saward
Music: Traditional
arr. D.G. Wilson

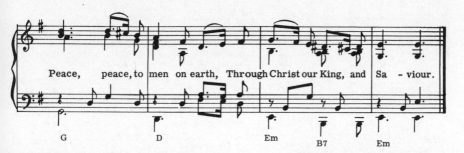

Peace, peace, to men on earth, Through Christ our King, and Sa - viour.

G   D   Em   B7   Em

2. His birth obscure, His family poor,
   He owned no crown, no kingdom.
   Yet men who grope in darkness, hope
   Since He brought light and freedom.
   Shame, Shame, and agony
   Though guiltless He of felony;
   Shout, Shout, His sinless name,
   Our Jesus, King and Saviour!

3. At fearful cost His life he lost
   That death might be defeated.
   The Man of Love, now risen above
   In majesty is seated.
   Low, Low, was His descent
   To men by sin and sorrow bent;
   Life, Life, to all who trust
   The Lord, our King and Saviour!

4. And all who trust will find they must
   Obey the will of heaven,
   For grief intense can make some sense
   To men who've been forgiven.
   Hard, Hard, the road He trod
   The Son of Man, the Son of God;
   Hope, Hope, in Christ alone,
   Our reigning King and Saviour!

189 O Let us sing

CHORUS:

Words and Music: L.C. Taylor

O, let us sing of our mer - ci - ful King,

G   G7   C

Migh- ty Re-deem- er is He;—— We give Him praise for His

G   A7   D7   G7

2. If you are weary and crushed with despair,
    When Satan's power is strong,
    Call to the One whom the foe must shun,
    He'll give you strength and a song!
        Chorus

3. He breaks the fetters of sorrow and sin,
    Raising men out of their plight,
    He calms the waves on the stormy sea,
    He turns the darkness to light.
        Chorus

4. He turns the wilderness into a well,
    The barren land into a plain,
    He makes the trusting and humble rejoice,
    Giving them gladness again.
        Chorus

190 Wonderful Jesus

Words: J.B. Foote
Music: G. Bailey

Won-der-ful Je - sus our Lord, won-der-ful King.

to you our prais-es out-poured, loud - ly we sing;

Trum-pet notes rich - ly scored, Strong beat and crashing chord,

For Je-sus Christ our Lord, our God and King.

2. Christ Jesus, Saviour and God, ruling on high,
   Lonely the pathway You trod, destined to die,
   Bearing our load of pain,
   Now gone above to reign,
   Glorious Son of God, Victor on high.

3. We praise You Jesus our Lord, Saviour and Friend,
   For You our thanks we record. Joy without end.
   Salvation's free reward,
   Pardon and peace restored,
   All from the Cross outpoured, wonderful Friend.

191 Christ the Light

Words: C. Idle
Music: N.L. Warren

Christ the Light who shines un- -fad- ing In the sad, sin darkened mind Guid - ing those who grope in er - ror Op-'ning eyes that sin made blind; Shows Himself the Lord of Glo - ry shin-ing

for a lost man - kind.

D7   G6   D   Bm   D   G6

2. Christ the Bread who came from Heaven
    Hungry souls to satisfy:
    Just as loaves must first be broken;
    Our Life-giver had to die;
        Made Himself a generous Offering,
        Gave Himself for our supply.

3. Christ the Life who rose in splendour
    From the cold and dismal cave.
    On the Resurrection-morning
    Conquered death and burst His grave;
        Showed Himself the mighty Champion,
        Still alive and strong to save.

4. Christ the King, to earth returning,
    Surely will not long delay;
    Christ the Son of God requires us
    Now to trust Him and obey;
        Stands Himself as Lord and Saviour,
        Asking our response today.

© C. Idle and N.L. Warren, 1969. By kind permission.

192 Hush little Baby

Words: P. Malloch
Music: Traditional
arr. D.G. Wilson

Hush little ba - by don't you cry,_____ Re -

D   Am7

-member Je-sus_____ You were born to die _____

D   G

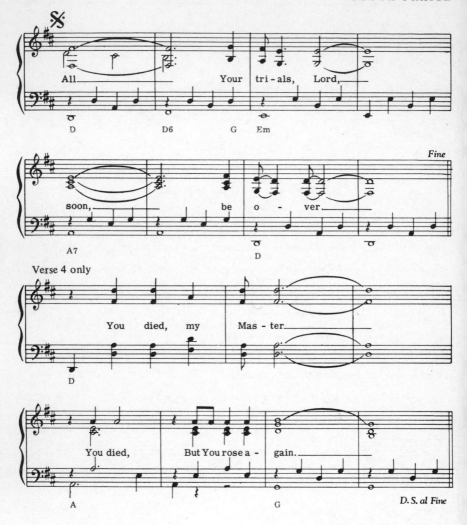

Verse 4 only

Fine

D. S. al Fine

2. To Your world You came, a Jew;
   But even they rejected You.
   All Your trials, Lord, soon be over.

3. On Your Cross You gave this cry,
   'My God, I am forsaken, why?'
   All Your trials, Lord, soon be over.

4. You died, my Master, You died,
   But You rose again.
   All Your trials, Lord, soon be over.

5. How can I so careless be,
   Of love which suffered so for me?
   All Your trials, Lord, soon be over.

6. Teach me, Lord, to love men too;
   If they laugh at me, they did worse to You
   All our trials, Lord, soon be over.

7. Work hard, my brothers, work fast,
   For He's coming soon.
   Then our trials, Lord, shall be over!

193 He is the Way

2. More of the Way - dear Lord, be this my choosing;
    More of the Truth - Lord, teach me day by day;
    More of the Life - for ever satisfying;
    More of Thyself - the Life, the Truth, the Way!

194 I know a name

Words and Music: K.W. Wood

1. I know a name That's nev-er gon-na pass a-way,
2. God said this name Would al-ways be re-membered here,
4. Then you will know The name that's never gon-na die,

Though men may try 'n try 'n try to for-get it,
Here in this world that turned Him a-way,
Then you'll be one of those who pray day by day,

God will nev-er let it die. Je-sus-that's the name
Men would always pray to Him. Je-sus-that's the name
One of those who say like me- Je-sus-that's the name

Son   of   God   who came   to die for   me.
He   who   took   the blame   for all my   sins,
Let   me spread   His fame   un-til He   comes,

D

To Coda ⊕

Last time

Je - sus-   that's   the   name.
Je - sus-   that's   the   name.
Je - sus-   that's   the   name.

D6   D7   G   C   D   D7

1   2

3. And do you

G   C   D   D   D7

know Him, this Je - sus, as your own liv-ing Lord?

Am   D7 G   C G

— If you want to know this Je-sus be - lieve His faith-ful

Am   D7   G   C G

word. If you call Him then be cer - tain that your

G   A   G6   Fmaj.7

voice will be heard, He'll come to you, make you

free.

CODA

195 There was a man

Words and Music: G. McClelland
arr. P. Bye

There was a man from Ga - li - lee He came to die for you and me. He gave His life on Cal - va - ry And now He lives for you and me. I know He lives in me.

F   C7   F   C7   F   C7   F   C7   F   Bb   F   Bb   F   Bb   F   C7   F   C7   F   G9   C9   C7   F

2. God sent His Son, His only one,
    To show us love from up above
    To show the way and how to pray
    And how He cares for us each day.
    I know He cares for me.

3. In such a world so full of sin
    Where can we find real peace within
    Where can we find our rock secure
    Where can we find a love so pure?
    Christ is the only one.

196 Jesus from glory

Words: J.E. Seddon
Music: M.A. Baughen and D.G. Wilson

Je - sus from glo - ry to Beth - le - hem came,

Born in a small wayside inn; He who cre - a - ted the

worlds by His pow'r In grace came to save us from sin.

2. Jesus the Word to His own people came,
    Their true Redeemer and King,
    Him they rejected, His truth they despised,
    They spurned all the gifts He would bring.

3. Jesus the Saviour to Calvary came,
    Victim of hatred and strife;
    Flogged and disowned He was nailed to a cross,
    And yet by that death we have life.

4. Jesus the Lord out of death's bondage came,
    Victor o'er Satan and sin,
    Now in His pow'r He will dwell in our lives,
    And help us our victory to win.

5. Jesus the Master to your life will come,
    Bringing salvation and peace;
    In His glad service you'll find your reward
    And pleasures that never shall cease.

6. Jesus the Sovereign in glory shall come,
    Man's full redemption to bring;
    Saints of all ages their Lord shall acclaim,
    Their Saviour, their God and their King.

197 There is no-one in the world like Jesus

Words: M.A. Baughen
Music: N.L. Warren

grac - ious Friend.   There is no - one in the

Eb6   D7

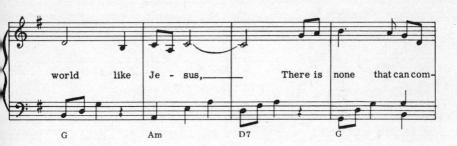

world   like   Je - sus,_____   There is none   that can com-

G   Am   D7   G

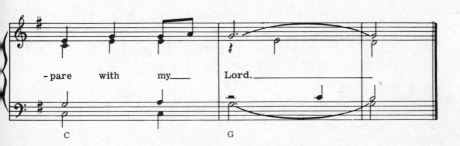

-pare   with   my___   Lord._____

C   G

2. If I go up to the heavens He is there
    If I go down to the depths He's there too
    Anywhere, everywhere,
    Anytime, all the time,
    He is with me evermore.
    Chorus

3. Nothing in this world can ever separate
    The believer from the love of the Lord.
    Death or life, evil powers,
    Present things, coming things,
    None can part us from His love.
    Chorus

198 King of kings

Words: D. Brand
Music: M.A. Baughen and N.L. Warren

King of kings and Prince of princes Greatest joy that came to earth Wondrous love our lives en-circling, Christ div-ine of ho-ly birth. On His knee___ He took the chil-dren At His feet the ox-en bowed, From His face there shone a rad-iance Brighter than the whit - est cloud.

2. With His precious blood He saved us,
   On His head He wore a thorn,
   By His hands He hung and suffered,
   Round Him was a cloak all torn.
   With the Father now in heaven,
   Jesus is enthroned on high,
   'Hallelujah', sing the angels,
   'See the King of kings is nigh!'

Incarnation and Birth
199 Lord of love

Words: T. Dudley-Smith
Music: N.L. Warren

2. Upon a cross my Saviour died,
    To ransom sinners crucified.
    His loving arms still open wide.
    All glory be to Jesus!

3. A victor's crown my Saviour won,
    His work of love and mercy done,
    The Father's high-ascended Son,
    All glory be to Jesus!

200 Holy Child

Words T. Dudley-Smith
Music: M.A. Baughen
arr. D.G. Wilson

Child,————— whose birth day brings Shep-herds

Am   D7

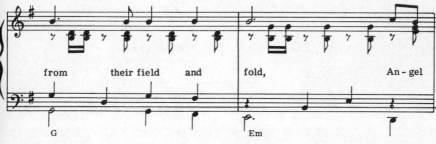

from   their field   and   fold,   An - gel

G   Em

choirs   and East - ern   kings,   Myrrh and

Am   Am7

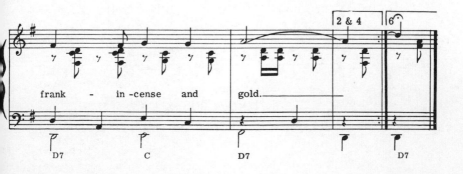

frank - in -cense   and   gold.—————————

D7   C   D7   D7

3. Holy Child, what gift of grace,
    From the Father freely willed
    In Your infant form we trace
    All God's promises fulfilled.

4. Holy Child, whose human years
    Span like ours delight and pain,
    One in human joys and tears,
    One in all but sin and stain.

5. Holy Child, so far from home,
    Sons of men to seek and save,
    To what dreadful death You come,
    To what dark and silent grave.

6. Holy Child, before whose Name
    Powers of darkness faint and fall;
    Conquered, death and sin and shame,
    Jesus Christ is Lord of all.

7. Holy Child, how still You lie-
    Safe the manger, soft the hay,
    Clear upon the Eastern sky
    Breaks the dawn of Christmas Day.

© T. Dudley-Smith and M.A. Baughen 1969. By kind permission.

201 Calypso carol

Words and Melody: M.A. Perry
arr.: S.K. Coates

See Him a-ly-ing on a bed of straw; A
draughty sta-ble with an o-pen door, Ma-ry cra-dl-ing the

babe she bore; The Prince of Glo-ry is His name.

2. Star of silver sweep across the skies,
    Show where Jesus in the manger lies.
    Shepherds swiftly from your stupor rise
    To see the Saviour of the world.
        Chorus

3. Angels, sing again the song you sang,
    Bring God's glory to the heart of man:
    Sing that Bethlehem's little baby can
    Be Salvation to the soul.
        Chorus

4. Mine are riches – from Thy poverty:
    From Thine innocence, eternity;
    Mine, forgiveness by Thy death for me,
    Child of sorrow for my joy.
        Chorus

© M.A. Perry 1969. By kind permission.

202 The road

Words: P. Monk
Music: M.A. Baughen

A ba - by was born in Beth - le - hem by a
stable light: a stranger in oc - cu - pied
coun - try on a win - ter night- But the
road runs from Beth - le - hem straight and sto - ny
steep and long: the road runs from

G C G D7 G
Am7 D7 G Em
Am7 Am D7 G D7
G Em Am7 D7 G C
Am7 D G Em

Beth - le - hem through thir - ty years to Cal - va - ry.

2. The baby born in Bethlehem
   Was Jesus Christ, God's Son,
   And when as man our Saviour came
   Redemption was begun -
     But the road runs...

3. For He was born in Bethlehem
   Under a winter sky
   To walk the road to Calvary
   There for our sins to die -
     And the road runs...

© P. Monk and M.A. Baughen, 1969. By kind permission.

203 O come, O come, Immanuel

Words from: The Great O Antiphons (12th - 13th cent.)
tr. J.M. Neale
Music: D.G. Wilson

O come, O come, Im - man - u - el, And ran - som cap - tive Is - ra - el, That mourns in lone - ly ex - ile here, Un - til the Son of God ap - pear.

2. O come, O come, Thou Lord of might
   Who to Thy tribes, on Sinai's height
   In ancient times didst give the law
   In cloud and majesty and awe:
      Refrain

3. O come, Thou rod of Jesse, free
   Thine own from Satan's tyranny;
   From depths of hell Thy people save,
   And give them victory o'er the grave:
      Refrain

4. O come, Thou Dayspring, come and cheer
   Our spirits by Thine advent here;
   Disperse the gloomy clouds of night,
   And death's dark shadows put to flight.
      Refrain

5. O come, Thou Key of David, come
   And open wide our heavenly home;
   Make safe the way that leads on high,
   And close the path to misery:
      Refrain

204 In between

Words: R.A. Leaver
Music: D.C. Jeffrey

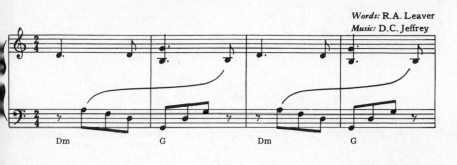

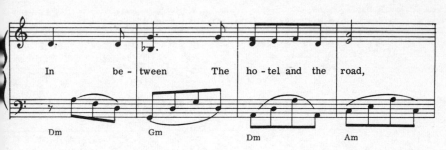

In be-tween The ho-tel and the road,

In a bor-rowed sta - ble The King comes as fore-told.____ The

man__ in the mid-dle is the one who came for us, As a

F   Dm9   F   Bb   Am   G

ba - by in a   cra - dle- And we   nailed Him to   a   cross.

2. In between
    A donkey and a cow,
    In a borrowed manger,
    The King descends so low.
        The man in the middle...

3. In between
    The husband and the wife,
    In a borrowed fam'ly
    The King takes on our life.
        The man in the middle...

4. In between
    The shepherds and the kings;
    Without the borrowed riches
    The King new value brings.
        The man in the middle...

5. In between
    Two crosses on a hill,
    On a borrowed gallows
    For us He pays the bill.
        The man in the middle...

© R.A. Leaver and D.C. Jeffrey, 1969. By kind permission.

205 The Lord of all glory

Words T. Dudley-Smith
Music: M.A. Baughen
arr. D.G. Wilson

F   C7   F   Dm   Gm7

Hush   you, my   ba - by,—   The   night   wind   is

C7   F   C7   F   Dm

cold.   The   lambs   from the   hill - side   Are

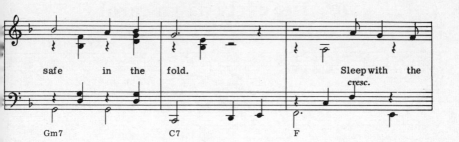

safe   in   the   fold.   Sleep with the
                                                    cresc.

Gm7   C7   F

star - light   And wake with   the   morn,

Dm   Am   Em   Am

ff The Lord of   all glo - ry   A ba-by is born.

D7   Gm   C7   F

2. Hush you, my baby,
    So soon to be grown,
    Watching by moonlight
    On mountain alone,
    Toiling and travelling -
    So sleep while you can,
    Till the Lord of all glory
    Is seen as a man.

3. Hush you, my baby,
    The years will not stay;
    The cross on the hilltop
    The end of the way.
    Dim through the darkness,
    In grief and in gloom,
    The Lord of all glory
    Lies cold in the tomb.

4. Hush you, my baby,
    The Father on high
    In power and dominion
    The darkness puts by.
    Bright from the shadows,
    The seal and the stone.
    The Lord of all glory
    Returns to His own.

5. Hush you, my baby,
    The sky turns to gold;
    The lambs from the hillside
    Are loose from the fold.
    Fast fades the midnight
    And new springs the morn,
    For the Lord of all glory
    A Saviour is born.

206 The early dawn carol

Words and Melody: S. Beckley
arr. M.C.T. Strover

grip of night___ had well-nigh gone,   In a sta - ble

bare___ in Ma - ry's care and Jo - seph's, There my Lord was

born.___   On a night like this,___ with its star - ry

sky,   Some shepherds had no time   to won - der

G

207 Christmas for God's holy people

Words: M. Saward
Music: M.A. Baughen
arr. D.G. Wilson

2. Child of Mary, virgin mother,
   Peasant baby, yet our king,
   Cradled once midst ass and oxen
   Joyful carols now we sing
   To our God....

3. Angel armies sang in chorus
   To our Christ's nativity
   He who came to share our nature
   So we sing with gaiety
   To our God....

4. Working men ran to the manger,
   Saw the babe of Bethlehem,
   Glorified the God of heaven,
   Now we join to sing with them
   To our God....

5. Infant lowly, born in squalor,
   Prophet, King and great High Priest
   Word of God to man descending
   Still we sing, both great and least
   To our God....

Cross and Resurrection
208 When I survey

Words: Isaac Watts
Music: O Waley, Waley, collected by Cecil J. Sharp.
arr. D.G. Wilson

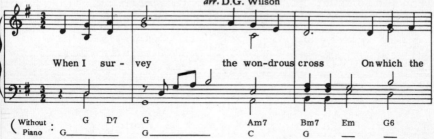

When I sur-vey the won-drous cross On which the

Prince of Glory died, My rich-est gain I count but

loss, And pour con-tempt on all my pride.

2. Forbid it, Lord, that I should boast
Save in the cross of Christ my God;
All the vain things that charm me most,
I sacrifice them to His blood.

3. See, from His head, His hands, His feet,
Sorrow and love flow mingled down;
Did e'er such love and sorrow meet,
Or thorns compose so rich a crown?

4. Were the whole realm of nature mine,
That were an offering far too small;
Love so amazing, so divine,
Demands my soul, my life, my all.

209 A man died

Words: D.E. Wood
Music: R.K. Price

VERSE
Freely adapt music for other verses

Long years a-go in a far East-ern land, a man died,___ Nails in His hands and His feet and a sword in His side,___ Crowds watched Him die, as He hung on a cross in the gloom. When they took Him down His bo-dy was sealed in a tomb.

2. The man had said 'after three days I rise from the dead' -
    His enemies the Jews now remembered what He had said.
    They wanted a guard for the tomb for they still feared the man,
    'Go your way', said Pilate, 'and make it as safe as you can.'
        Chorus

3. So soldiers set watch on the tomb all day and all night,
    And on the third day, the women came ere it was light,
    They found the tomb open, no soldiers, the body was gone,
    And inside were two angels who said 'He is risen - God's Son'.
        Chorus

4. The Jews did not find Him, and death could not hold Him, nor the grave,
    For this man is Jesus, Messiah, Almighty to save.
    He was mocked by the crowd, as He died on the cross for their sin,
    But He rose from the dead, a sure hope for all now to win.
        Chorus

5. What is He to you, this Jesus who died in such shame?
    Your Saviour? a good man? or merely a story-book name?
    Own Him as your Saviour, your lips with His praises will ring,
    For one day you must meet Him, as either your Judge or your King.
        Chorus

210 On a hill called Skull

Words: R. Warren
Music: G. Wilson
arr: G.R.Timms

3. On the tree on the Hill called Skull.
   Christ Jesus won the fight,
   The Battle then was with Hell,
   So day turned black as night.

4. Not that we knew or asked Him to
   In fact we put Him there
   Yes, the man
   On the tree of the Hill called Skull,
   Who stripped the Devil bare.

5. On the tree on the Hill called Skull,
   Christ Jesus ripped apart,
   That veil which cuts us off from God,
   Our selfish wilful heart.

6. Not that we touch or even reached,
   For the friendship of our God
   In the man
   On the tree on the Hill called Skull,
   Whose nail-pierced hand says 'Come'.

7. On the tree on the Hill called Skull,
   Christ Jesus once for all,
   Put the world to rights that hour,
   'It's finished' was His last call.

8. Not that we wanted it quite that free
   With nothing more to pay
   To the man
   On the tree on the Hill called Skull,
   Whose death gives life today.

211 A hill beside Jerusalem

Words: C.E. Reddin and R.K. Price
Music: R.K. Price

A hill be - side Je - ru - sa - lem, Three

Dm   Am7   Bb   Dm

cross - es stark and free, Mark the place where three men

Dm   C   F   Bb   Gm

slow - ly died-And One there died for you and me.__

Am7   Bb6   Dm   Am7   Bb   Dm

2. They hailed Him at Jerusalem's gate,
   And gathered there to see
   The Son of God come riding in -
   But there He died for you and me.

3. A friend betrayed Him to the Jews,
   But death He would not flee;
   They scorned and mocked and spat on Him,
   And there He died for you and me.

4. They led Him up to Calvary's hill,
   And nailed Him to a tree,
   They pierced His side with cruel spear -
   And there He died for you and me.

5. But death our Saviour could not hold,
   For God's own Son was He,
   He rose victorious over sin,
   Because He died for you and me.

212 Do you remember?

Words and Music: The Crossbeats
arr. J. and B. Courtie

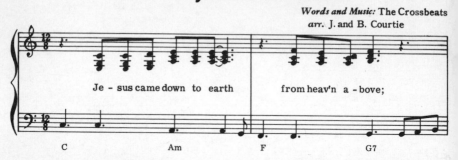

Je - sus came down to earth   from heav'n a - bove;

C   Am   F   G7

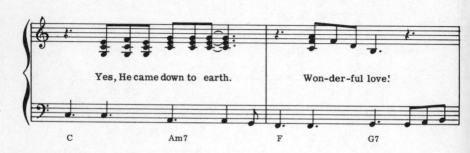

Yes, He came down to earth.   Won-der-ful love!

C   Am7   F   G7

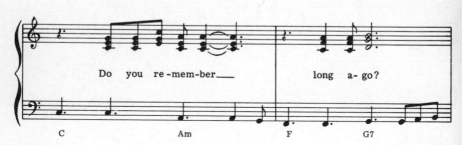

Do   you   re-mem-ber___   long   a- go?

C   Am   F   G7

Do   you   re- mem-ber,___   He loved us so.

C   Am   F   G7

Verse:

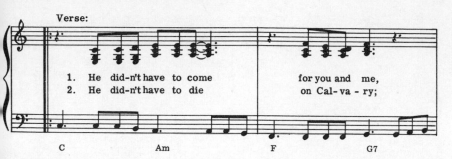

1. He did-n't have to come for you and me,
2. He did-n't have to die on Cal-va-ry;

C Am F G7

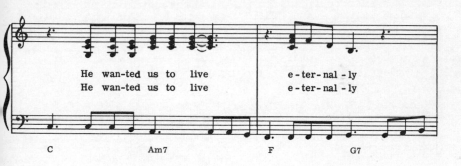

He wan-ted us to live e-ter-nal-ly
He wan-ted us to live e-ter-nal-ly

C Am7 F G7

Do you re-mem-ber tho' you weren't there?
Do you re-mem-ber long,— a - go?

C Am F G7

Do you re-mem-ber, or don't you care, don't you
Do you re-mem-ber, He loved us so, loved us

C Am F G

care? _____
so! _____ Is it noth-ing to you that Je-sus

Am   G7   F   D7

died? _____ Is it noth-ing that He was cru-ci-

G   E7

-fied?   Can't you be-lieve?

A   G   E

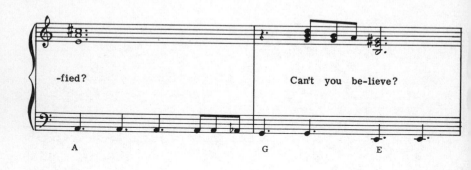

Can't you be-lieve?

F   D   G   G   G7

Do you re-mem-ber,____ tho' you weren't there?

C   Am   F   G

Do you re-mem-ber____ or don't you care?____ Don't you

C   Am   F   G7

care,____ don't you care,____ don't you care____ don't you care? Do you re-

C   Am   F   G7

-member?____

C   Am   F   Db7   C

213 A purple robe

Words: T. Dudley-Smith
Music: D.G. Wilson

1. A pur - ple robe, a crown of thorn, A
4. He hangs, by whom the world was made, Be-

Dm   Gm   C

reed in His right hand; Be -
-neath the dark - ened sky; The

Dm   Am   Dm

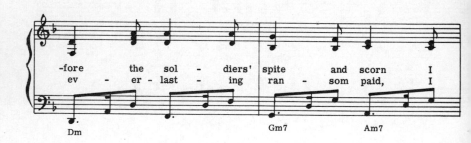

-fore the sol - diers' spite and scorn I
ev - er - last - ing ran - som paid, I

Dm   Gm7   Am7

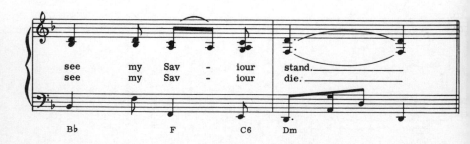

see my Sav - iour stand.
see my Sav - iour die.

Bb   F   C6   Dm

2. He bears be - tween - the Ro - man guard The
5. He shares on high His Fa - ther's throne, Who

Am Dm Am

weight of all____ our woe;_____ A
once in mer - cy came;_____ For

C Dm6 Em7 A(sus.4) A

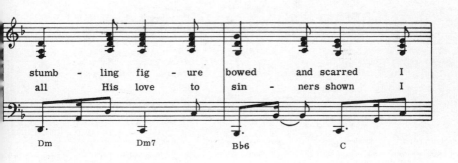

stumb - ling fig - ure bowed and scarred I
all His love to sin - ners shown I

Dm Dm7 Bb6 C

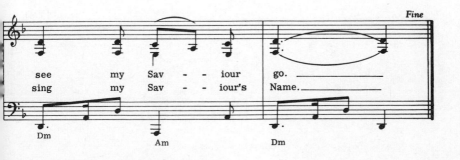

see my Sav - - iour go. _____
sing my Sav - - iour's Name.____

Dm Am Dm

Fine

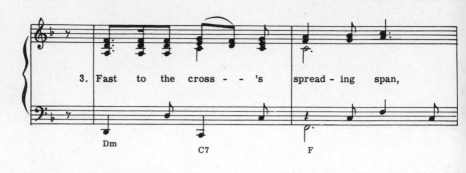

3. Fast to the cross - - 's spread - ing span,

Dm   C7   F

High in the sun - lit air,

Dm   Am   Dm

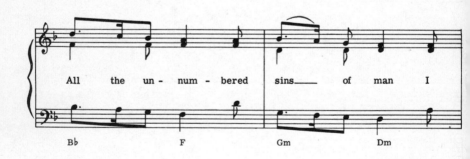

All the un - num - bered sins____ of man I

Bb   F   Gm   Dm

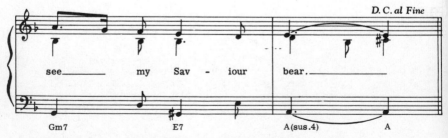

D. C. al Fine

see____ my Sav - iour bear.____

Gm7   E7   A(sus.4)   A

© T. Dudley–Smith 1968 and D. G. Wilson 1969. By kind permission.

214 O Sacrifice of Calvary

Words: M. Saward
Music: W.J. Walter

O Sac - ri - fice of Cal -var - y, O Lamb whose sa - cred
blood was shed, O great High Priest on heav-en's throne, O
Vic - tor from the dead. Here I re-call Your ag - o -
- ny Here see a - gain Your blood stained brow Be - yond the
sign of Bread and Wine I know Your pres - ence now.

2. No longer, Saviour, do You plead
    Your glorious sacrifice unique,
    Yet Lord, in heaven intercede
    While I Your mercy seek.
    Before Your Holy Table laid
    I kneel once more in love and peace,
    Your Blood and Flesh my soul refresh
    With joy that shall not cease.

215 'This do', the Master said

Words: M. Saward
Music: M.A. Baughen
arr. D.G. Wilson

H

2. Don't come, if you would boast
    Your knowledge and your might,
    Don't come, if you refuse
    To serve the Lord of Light.
    But those whose sin
    Has been confessed
    May take their rest
    And join herein.

3. For you, whose sin He bore
    A promise He provides,
    His covenant He makes
    And at His board presides.
    His Sacrifice
    He'll not repeat,
    But take and eat,
    And count the price.

4. One loaf, one body, we,
    One family divine,
    In sweet communion feed
    Upon that Bread and Wine.
    The Great High Priest,
    Until He come
    Has now become
    Our heavenly feast.

5. Then lift Your Church to heaven
    Where hunger is no more,
    And through eternity,
    O Christ, we shall adore.
    So make us share
    In glad embrace
    Your matchless grace,
    Both here and there.

© M. Saward 1962 and M.A. Baughen 1969. By kind permission.

216 The third morning

Words: D. Brand
Music: A. Durden

Bright   dawned the morn-ing on Geth - se - ma-ne's   cave,

Cm   Fm7   G

Ma - ry Mag - da - lene   came to   weep   at   the grave.

Cm   Fm7   G   Cm

What did she find when she came, full of care? The
stone rolled a - way, and her Mas- ter not there!

Refrain:

Ma - ry, Ma - ry weep-ing at the tomb, Je - sus came and

took a - way her gloom. Je - sus came and took a - way her gloom.

D.C. last time only

2. 'Where have they taken Him?' poor Mary did pray,
    Crying, and bowing her head in dismay;
    Suddenly in front of her a shadow did fall,
    Mary raised her eyes - 'tis the gardener, that's all.'
    Chorus
3. 'Why are you weeping? Come, tell me your fears.'
    'My Jesus is gone', she said through her tears.
    'Mary!' was all that the Person replied,
    Then Mary knew at once that her Lord had not died.
    Chorus
4. Overcome with joy, she touched the hem of His gown,
    Clinging to Jesus, at His feet she fell down.
    'Lord, you're alive!' was all that Mary could say,
    'This is indeed your Resurrection Day!'
    Chorus

© D. Brand and A. Durden 1969. By kind permission.

217 It happened in Jerusalem

Words: P. Monk
Music: M.A. Baughen
arr: D.G. Wilson

It hap-pened in Je-ru-sa-lem__ in the ear-ly spring they

say, God lived and died a man or some such cra-zy thing: For it

hap-pened ve-ry long a-go and ve-ry far a-way, 1-6: It
7: But

hap-pened much too long a-go to make a scrap of sense to -
though it hap-pened long a-go__

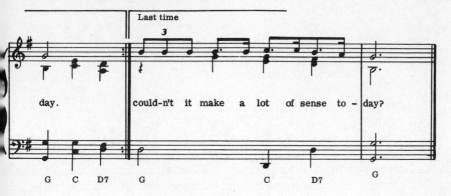

2. The charge they brought was blasphemy,
    The prisoner was framed,
    And Pilate washed his hands of him -
    But why should he be blamed:
    Chorus

3. They flogged him then and mocked him,
    And dragged him to the Hill
    Through jostling crowds that jeered -
    But why be troubled still:
    Chorus

4. And on that city rubbish-tip
    They nailed him to a cross
    And left him in the sun to die -
    But what's all that to us?
    Chorus

5. Friends left him through the sabbath day
    In a borrowed grave,
    On Sunday morning he had gone -
    But still what does that prove:
    Chorus

6. Alive they say he joined these friends
    And all the nail-marks saw;
    He parted from them heavenwards -
    But how can we be sure:
    Chorus

7. It happened in Jerusalem
    In the early spring;
    They say, God lived and died a man -
    Or some such crazy thing;
    Chorus

218 We shall rise

The group can be divided for this song, so that one half
is singing the chorus while the other half is singing a
verse, and then vice versa.

Words: Anon
Music: Traditional
arr: J.D. Thornton

We shall then be with Him ev - er - more.

C   G7

We shall then be with the Lord,   We shall then be with the Lord.

C   C7   F   F#

We   shall then   be with Him   ev - er - more.

C   G7   C

2. Death has lost its sting for us
    Death has lost its sting for us
    Death has lost its sting for evermore
        (repeat)
    Chorus

3. Hallelujahs then will ring
    Hallelujahs then will ring
    Hallelujahs to the Lamb who died
        (repeat)
    Chorus

The Holy Spirit
219 Spirit of God within me

Words T. Dudley-Smith
Music: M.A. Baughen
arr. D.G. Wilson

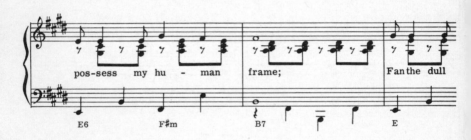

Spir-it of God with-in me,

pos-sess my hu-man frame;   Fan the dull

em-bers   of   my heart   Stir up the liv-ing

flame.   Strive till that im-age

Ad - am lost, New min - ted and re - stored

F#   B7   E   C#m   F#m   B7

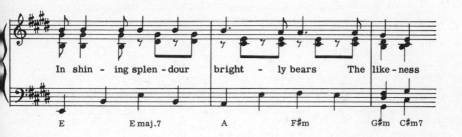

In shin - ing splen - dour bright - ly bears The like - ness

E   E maj.7   A   F#m   G#m   C#m7

vv 1-3   v4

of____ the Lord.   day.

F#m   B7   E   E

2. Spirit of truth within me,
   Possess my thought and mind;
   Lighten anew the inward eye
   By Satan rendered blind;
   Shine on the words that wisdom speaks
   And grant me power to see
   The truth made known to men in Christ,
   And in that truth be free.

3. Spirit of love within me,
   Possess my hands and heart;
   Break through the bonds of self-concern
   That seeks to stand apart:
   Grant me the love that suffers long,
   That hopes, believes and bears,
   The love fulfilled in sacrifice,
   That cares as Jesus cares.

4. Spirit of life within me,
   Possess this life of mine;
   Come as the wind of heaven's breath,
   Come as the fire divine!
   Spirit of Christ, the living Lord,
   Reign in my house of clay,
   Till from its dust with Christ I rise
   To everlasting day.

220 Fire of God

Words: M. Saward
Music: D.G. Wilson

Fire of God, ti-tan-ic Spir - it,

Burn with - in our hearts to - day,

Cleanse our sin; may we ex - hib - it

Ho - li - ness in ev - 'ry way.

Purge the squal- id - ness that shames us,

Soils the bo - dy; taints the soul.

A7   D

And through Je - sus Christ who claims us,

Dm   Dm7   G7   G9   Em   G7   C maj.9   C

Last time

Pu - ri - fy us; make us whole.

F   F maj.7   C   Dm7   G7
                                      C

2. Wind of God, dynamic Spirit,
   Breathe upon our hearts today
   That we may Your power inherit
   Hear us, Spirit, as we pray.
   Fill the vacuum that enslaves us,
   Emptiness of heart and soul,
   And, through Jesus Christ who saves us,
   Give us life and make us whole.

3. Voice of God, prophetic Spirit,
   Speak to every heart today,
   To encourage or prohibit,
   Urging action or delay.
   Clear the vagueness which impedes us,
   Come, enlighten mind and soul.
   And, through Jesus Christ who leads us,
   Teach the truth that makes us whole.

221 He's the Comforter

Words and Music: R.T. Bewes
arr. M.C.T. Strover

He was there when earth was hurled in space, By
man or beast un-trod. He was mov-ing ov-er the
wa-ter's face, The un-seen Spir-it of God.
CHORUS He's the
Com-for-ter, He's the breath of God, He's the
wind of rushing mighty pow'r. He gives strength to win When He

dwells with - in Mak-ing Je - sus real ev-'ry hour.

C6   Am7   C   D7   G6

2. He was there of old and gave God's Word.
   Inspired both sage and youth;
   The apostles wrote what they'd seen and heard,
   Led by the Spirit of Truth.
        Chorus

3. He was there in fire on the Church outpoured,
   His gifts and power sufficed;
   He reminded men of their reigning Lord,
   The living Spirit of Christ.
        Chorus

4. He is here to give new birth, and still
   The clamour and the strife;
   Let us grieve Him not but seek His will,
   Dynamic Spirit of Life!
        Chorus

© R.T. Bewes 1968. By kind permission.

222 If you've asked

Words and Music: D.B. Pettinger

1. If you've asked my Je - sus___ To be your Sav - iour___

C   G7 C7   F   Bb C7   F

___ You will know the Spir - it's pow'r with - in.

Dm Am Gm C7   G7 C7   F

He will want to change you___ To make you like your Lord___

C   G7 C7   F   Bb   F A7 Dm

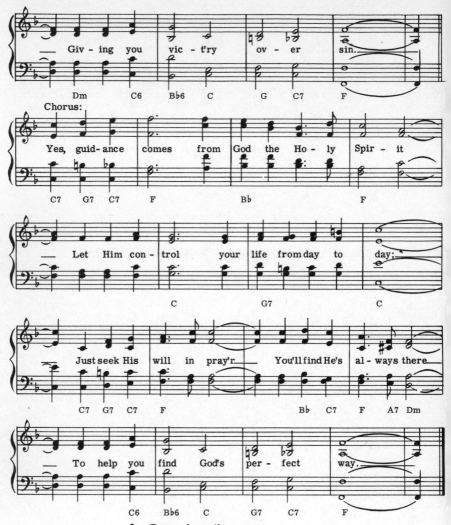

2. Do you know the answer
    To all the problems
    You may have to face this very day?
    Jesus sent His Spirit
    To live within your heart
    To hear and guide you when you pray.
        Chorus

3. Is your life as useful
    As God desires it?
    Is He satisfied with all you do?
    Seek the Spirit's guidance
    And He will show you all
    The Lord your God has planned for you.
        Chorus

The Second Coming
223 When the Lord

Words: T. Dudley-Smith
Music: M.A. Baughen and D.G. Wilson

1. When the Lord in glory comes

Not the trumpets, not the drums,

Not the anthem, not the psalm, Not the

thun - der, not the calm,

2. When the Lord is seen again
   Not the glories of His reign,
   Not the lightnings through the storm,
   Not the radiance of His form,
   Not His pomp and power alone,
   Not the splendours of His throne,
   Not His robe and diadems,
   Not the gold and not the gems,
   But His face upon my sight
   Shall be darkness into light -
     But His face upon my sight
     Shall be darkness into light.

3. When the Lord to human eyes
   Shall bestride our narrow skies,
   Not the child of humble birth,
   Not the carpenter of earth,
   Not the man by men denied,
   Not the victim crucified,
   But the God who died to save,
   But the victor of the grave,
   He it is to whom I fall,
   Jesus Christ, my All in all -
     He it is to whom I fall,
     Jesus Christ, my All in all.

I

224 He's coming

Words and Music: The Crossbeats
arr: J. and B. Courtie

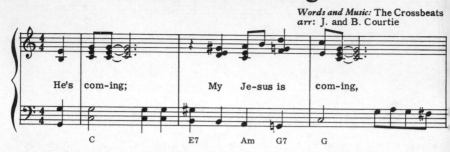

He's com-ing; My Je-sus is com-ing,

C   E7   Am   G7   G

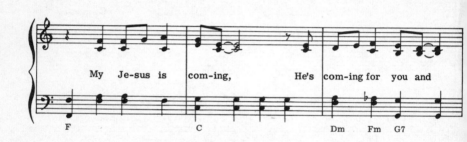

My Je-sus is com-ing, He's com-ing for you and

F   C   Dm   Fm   G7

me. When He went a-way He told us to

Am   G7   C   E7   Am   G7

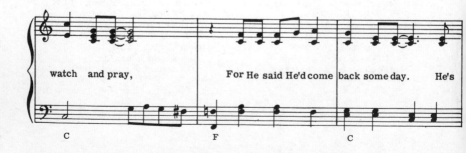

watch and pray, For He said He'd come back some day. He's

C   F   C

com-ing for you and me.   He's coming a-gain.

Dm Fm G7   C   C7   F

Can't you see   that He died for you   and He died for me?   He

              C

wants us to live   e- ter- nal - ly. So if heav-en's   not your

F   Dm

home,— You can take Him   as   your   own.   He's com-ing;

G   Dm   G7   C

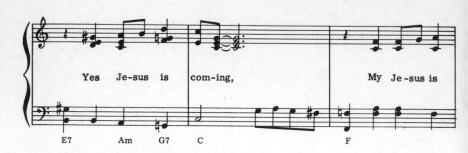

Yes Je-sus is com-ing, My Je-sus is

E7   Am   G7   C   F

To ⊕ Coda

com-ing, He's coming for you and me. In that

C   Dm Fm G7   C   G7

sud-den hour We shall see Him in all His pow'r.

C   E7   Am C7   C

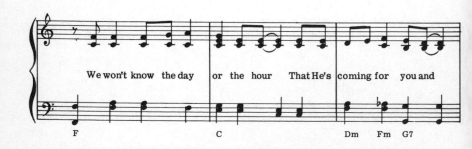

We won't know the day or the hour That He's coming for you and

F   C   Dm Fm G7

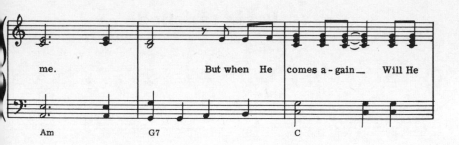

me.   But when He   comes a-gain__   Will He

Am   G7   C

take you then, Or will He   leave you here   with oth-er men? Now are you

E7   Am   G7   C   F

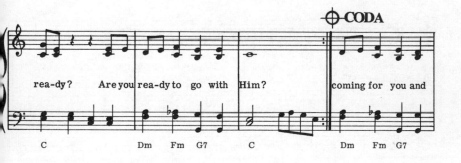

CODA

rea-dy?   Are you rea-dy to   go with   Him?   coming for you and

C   Dm   Fm G7   C   Dm   Fm   G7

me.   He's coming for   you   and   me.

Am   Dm   Fm   G7   C   C6

225 Is He satisfied?

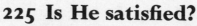

Is   He sat-is - fied with me?_____

Have   I done my best,   have   I stood the test?

Is   He sat - is - fied with   me? _____   When my

Lord shall come a - gain,   When He   walks and   talks with

THE SECOND COMING 135

226 When He comes

Words: T. Dudley-Smith
Music: J.D. Thornton

1. When He comes When He comes We shall see the Lord in glo - ry when He comes, As I read the gos-pel sto-ry We shall see the Lord in glo-ry, We shall see the Lord in glo - ry when He comes! With the

2. When He comes,
    When He comes,
    We shall hear the trumpet sounded when He comes,
    We shall hear the trumpet sounded,
    See the Lord by saints surrounded,
    We shall hear the trumpet sounded when He comes!
        With the Alleluias ringing to the sky,
        With the Alleluias ringing to the sky,
        We shall hear the trumpet sounded,
        See the Lord by saints surrounded,
        With the Alleluias ringing to the sky!

3. When He comes,
    When He comes,
    We shall all rise up to meet Him when He comes,
    When He calls His own to greet Him
    We shall all rise up to meet Him,
    We shall all rise up to meet Him when He comes.
        With the Alleluias ringing to the sky,
        With the Alleluias ringing to the sky,
        When He calls His own to greet Him,
        We shall all rise up to meet Him,
        With the Alleluias ringing to the sky.

4. Repeat verse 1

© T. Dudley-Smith and J.D. Thornton 1969. By kind permission.

227 Jesus shall return

Words: P. Monk
Music: M.A. Baughen
arr: M.C.T. Strover

an-gels   And the songs   of suns and   plan-ets   And

Bb

G7

C7

ev - 'ry voice in Cre- a - tion shall be   His wel-come   then.

F   Fmaj.7   F7   D7   G   C7   F

2.   Once He had a human birth
     And lived like us upon this earth
     Knew human grief and human mirth:
         But. . but. . He shall return in glory
         But. . but. . He shall return as King-
     And sorrow banished for ever,
     And joy multiplied for ever,
     And human laughter in heaven,
     Shall be His fanfare then.

3.   Once He suffered human pain,
     Felt sun and wind, the storm and rain,
     Tempted like us again and again
         But. . but. . He shall return in glory
         But. . but. . He shall return as King-
     And the earth become His footstool,
     And the sun a gem in His crown,
     And Satan thrown down defeated,
     Shall be His trophies then.

4.   Once He passed through agony
     Knew conflict in Gethsemane
     Then hung exposed, nailed to a tree:
         But. . but. . He shall return in glory
         But. . but. . He shall return as King-
     And all knees shall bow in His name
     Every tongue confess Him as Lord,
     And all His children around Him
     Shall be His victory then.

Missionary and Social Concern
228 People I meet

Words and Music: M. Whitten

When I look a-round me This is the truth I see Peo-ple are
suff - 'ring the whole world through. I look the oth-er way,
Think of my-self a-lone, Knowing what I ought to do.

2. When I have this world's goods -
   Standards of living high
   One of the 'haves' rather than the 'have-nots',
   Grant me the grace to give,
   Open my heart in love,
   Tackling the world's trouble spots.

3. Help me to feed the hungry
   And give the thirsty drink.
   Caring for strangers and those alone.
   Help me to visit all
   Those who may need a call
   Helping some to make a home.

4. When the Son of Man comes,
   All nations gathered there,
   To those He welcomes He then will say,
   'I assure you that your deed
   To my brothers in their need
   Was a deed you did to Me'.

229 Send the collecting man from your gate

Words and Music: G. H. Reid
arr: D.G. Wilson

1. Sit -ting right there in your two - car home Watching the world go by; Watch-ing the ref - u - gees still roam See-ing the hun- gry die. But there's nothing you can do You simp- ly say: I haven't got mon-ey to throw a - way

(Adapt rhythm to fit words vv2 & 3)

Send the col - lect - ing man from your gate 'But

C7   F6   F

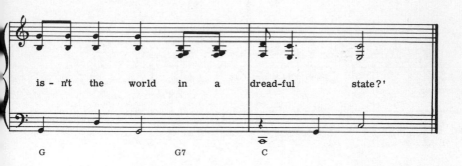

is - n't the world in a dread-ful state?'

G   G7   C

2. Sitting right there in your sprung settee
    Watching the TV show
    Seeing the struggle to set men free
    Watching it blow-by-blow.
    But the cost of living is getting you down
    You can't even spare a half-a-crown.
    Send the collecting man from your gate
    'But isn't the world in a dreadful staté'.

3. Sitting right there in your favourite chair
    After a three-course meal
    Seeing the suffering everywhere
    Watching the wealthy steal.
    But your rates go up and they freeze your pay
    You can't get abroad for your holiday
    Send the collecting man from your gate
    'But isn't the world in a dreadful state?'

230 Black or white, sir

Words and Music : G. C. H. Roberts arr. M. Atkin

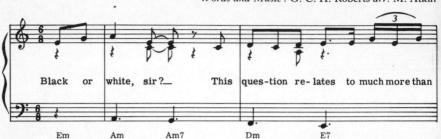

Black or white, sir?— This ques-tion re-lates to much more than

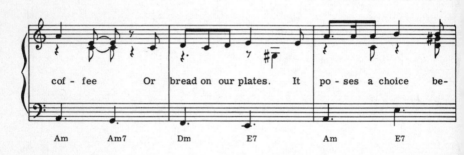

cof - fee Or bread on our plates. It po - ses a choice be-

-tween two ex-tremes Af - fec-ting the mem-bers of our tour-ing teams; De-

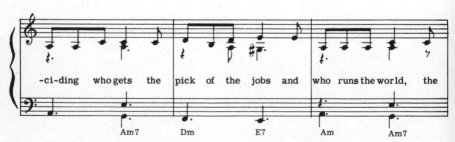

-ci-ding who gets the pick of the jobs and who runs the world, the

'wogs' or the 'nobs'. It's as fier-y as touchwood, we can-not ig-nore, or think all we need is a change in the law; It's men's hearts that dif-fer, some warm and some cold, What-ev-er the col-our of skin we be-hold.

D.C.

2. Love or hate, sir?
I ask you to say;
Please do not take long now,
There's no middle way;
Just think if you'd happened to be born jet black -
You'd want men to pay you, not give you the sack;
Remember who carried the cross of our Lord:
For he was an African forced by a sword;
There won't be a conflict in Britain's small land,
If different races can live hand-in-hand;
When we get to heaven, without any doubt,
No skin will be there to point us all out!

231 The people in between

Words adapted: from an original poem by
an undergraduate of Clare College, Cambridge.
Music: M.A. Baughen

1. In the Mis - sion near the front, all is
qui - et: it is night: Then the guns be-hind the house be-gin to
pound and in their light The man - y huts of straw, the frightened
fa -ces can be seen, — The fa-ces of the Peo-ple In Be-tween.

2. They have left their mountain dwellings, where they could no longer stay:
    They are sick and they are weary, and their children die each day,
    For there's little rice to eat, and no way of keeping clean -
    No comfort for the People In Between.

3. These people are not fighting men, they're labourers by birth
    They only wished for peace, to share the good things of the Earth.
    But their cattle disappeared, and the crops were brown, not green -
    No living for the People In Between.

4. What do they know of politics, the clash of East and West?
    Both promising the people that 'Our side can serve you best'
    But while the war drags on, it seems that neither side is keen
    To stop, and help the People In Between.

5. The Hospital is crowded, and the orderlies are few:
    They carry on because they know they have a job to do.
    A Minister was killed last week, a man of God who'd been
    Just trying to help the People In Between.

6. When fighting is the order, then the money's always there
    But those who offer comfort find that Governments don't care,
    It's up to you and me to help, and show them that we mean
    Our pity for the People In Between.

© Music by M.A. Baughen 1969 By kind permission.

232 Tell all the world about Jesus

Words: J.E. Seddon
Music: W.J. Walter

His sal - va - tion sing. Tell all men of His

Bb F C7 A7 Dm G7 C7

great - - -ness, In na - ture and in grace; Cre-

F Dm G7 C7 A7 Dm C7

-a - tor and re - deem - er, The Lord of time and space.

F A7 Dm Am7 D7 Gm Dm C7 F

2. Tell all the world about Jesus,
That men in Him may find
The joy of His forgiveness,
True peace of heart and mind.
Tell all men of His goodness,
His deep, unfailing care;
Of love so rich in mercy,
A love beyond compare.

3. Tell all the world about Jesus,
That everyone may know
Of His almighty triumph
O'er every evil foe.
Tell all men of His glory,
When sin is overthrown,
And He shall reign in splendour,
The King upon His throne.

233 Is there an answer

Words and Music: The Kinsmen

arr: The Settlers and M.C.T. Strover

Intro:

8va
E   G#m7   A6   B

CHORUS

Is there an ans-wer to it all?
E   G#m   F#m   B7

Is there an ans-wer to it all?
E   G#m   F#m   B

Can we feel at all re - spon - si-ble?
E   G#m   F#m   B7

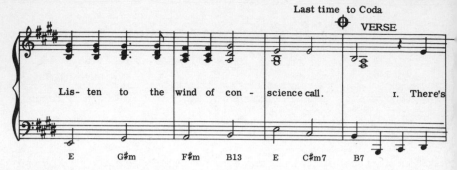

Last time to Coda   VERSE

Lis- ten to the wind of con - science call.   1. There's

E   G#m   F#m   B13   E   C#m7   B7

two thirds of the world   go hun- gry ev - 'ry night,

E   C#m

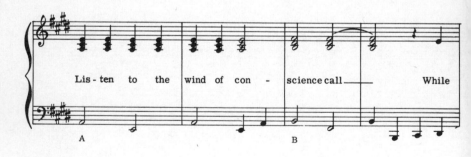

Lis- ten to the wind of con - science call_____   While

A   B

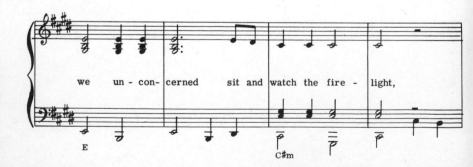

we un - con - cerned   sit and watch the fire - light,

E   C#m

2. A man has to fight to gain his civil right,
Listen to the wind of conscience call,
While we unconcerned sit and watch the firelight,
Is there an answer to it all?
Chorus

3. They crucified a man because they thought He might
Make us listen to the wind of conscience call.
While we unconcerned sit and watch the firelight,
And He is the answer to it all.

Chorus
He is the answer to it all, He is the answer to it all,
We can all be so responsible,
He is the answer to it all;
We can all be so responsible,
Listen to the wind of conscience call.

234 As for our world

Words: T. Dudley-Smith
Music: M.A. Baughen
arr. D.G. Wilson

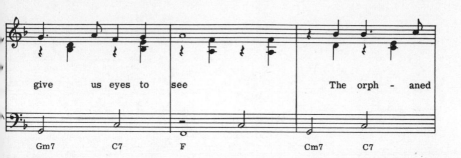

give us eyes to see The orph - aned

Gm7   C7   F   Cm7   C7

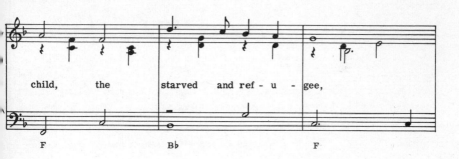

child,   the   starved   and ref - u - gee,

F   Bb   F

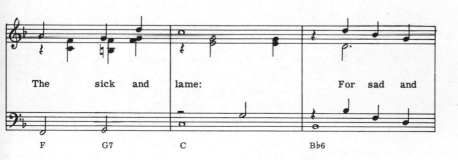

The   sick   and   lame: For sad   and

F   G7   C   Bb6

need - - y   chil - dren ev - 'ry - where___

F   Dm   Gm7   C7   F

For this our world,   we lift   our

F7   Bb   Gm

hands   in   pray'r.

C7

2. As for our world we lift our hearts in praise,
    The joy of home with lights and hearth ablaze,
        The welcome plain;
    So we recall the homeless and the cold,
    The destitute, the prisoners, and the old
        Who lie in pain:
    For all who grieve, for all who know despair -
    For this our world, we lift our hands in prayer.

3. As for our world we lift our hearts in praise,
    Recount the blessings that our life displays
        In every part,
    So look in mercy, Lord, where shadows rest,
    The ravaged homes by want and wars oppressed,
        The sick at heart.
    With burdens more than man was meant to bear -
    For this our world, we lift our hands in prayer.

4. As for our world we lift our hearts in praise,
    The love of God on all our works and ways,
        So we commend
    All those who loveless live and hopeless mourn,
    Who die at last uncomforted, forlorn,
        Without a friend;
    Who own no Saviour's love, no Father's care -
    For this our world, we lift our hands in prayer.

5. As for our world we lift our hearts in praise,
    So with our songs of thankfulness we raise
        This ageless plea:
    That darkened souls who have no song to sing
    May find in Christ the living Lord and King
        He came to be;
    And in His cross and resurrection share -
    For this our world, we lift our hands in prayer.

Prayer and the Word

235 Meet the Saviour

Prayerfully

Words and Music: G. Brattle

Meet Je - sus in the morn - ing, As day is breaking through; Meet Je - sus in the noon - tide, He'll talk a - gain with you; Meet Je - sus in the ev - 'ning, As thoughts are turned to rest; Be sure to meet the Sav - iour, And ev - 'ry day is blest!

236 An all-day faith

Words: D. Brand
Music: A. Durden

It's an all day faith you must have in your Lord, It's an
all day faith you must have in your Lord, It's an all day faith you must
have in your Lord, For He loves you all the day
long. loves you all the day long.

A little slower

Verse: (Solo)

In the quiet of the morn - ing give some time to Him,

E   C#m   F#m7   B7

Pray-ing that He will en - rich you with-in, For - give and de-li-ver you from

A   E   B7   E   G#m

all of your sin Yes the morn-ing you must give to your Lord.

E7   A7   E   F#m7   E6   B7   E A E

2.   In the heat of the noon-day put your faith in your God,
        Knowing that He's there as your Staff and your Rod,
        As you walk in the Way, tread the steps that He trod;
        Yes, the noon-day you must give to your Lord.
        Chorus

3.   In the cool of the evening commune with the Son,
        Telling Him all about all you have done.
        Sharing your sorrows and recounting your fun;
        Yes, the evening you must give to your Lord.
        Chorus

237 Hands of Jesus

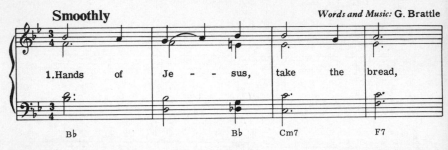

Words and Music: G. Brattle

Smoothly

1.Hands   of   Je - - sus,   take   the   bread,

Bb   Bb   Cm7   F7

As   long   a - go   While   here   be - low;

Bb   C7   F7

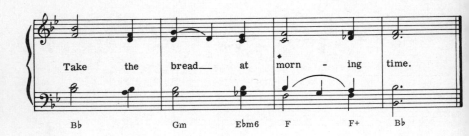

Take   the   bread___   at   morn - ing   time.

Bb   Gm   Ebm6   F   F+   Bb

2. Hands of Jesus, bless the bread;
    Bless it to me,
    That it may be
    Living bread at morning time.

3. Hands of Jesus, break the bread,
    And break it small,
    And grant to all
    Broken bread at morning time.

4. Hands of Jesus, give the bread,
    That with Thy Word,
    We may be fed;
    Hear our prayer at morning time.

* **The word 'evening' may be used when applicable.**

238 Open my ears

Based on words by: S.N. Davies
Music: J.A. Cox

1. Op - en my ears to Your Word
Lord of my life, I pray,——
That as I seek to serve You
I may hear what You say.

2.	Open my eyes to Your Word
That as I read each day,
New things I may discover
To help me walk Your way.

3.	Open my heart to Your Word
That as I read today
My heart may not be hardened
But will with joy obey.

239   Kingdoms may rise

Words and Music: J. Lorimer Gray and D. Kennedy
arr: D.G. Wilson

King-doms may rise   Kingdoms may fall   Na-tions re-fuse to

A   A7

hear God's call   But the   word of the   Lord en - du-reth   for ev - er-

D   E7

-more._____   Things that we   love

A   D   A   D   A

last for a   day   Then in the morn-ing   fade a - way   But the

A7   D

word of the Lord en - du -reth for ev - er - more.

E7   A   D

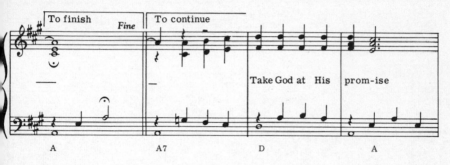

To finish   *Fine*   To continue

Take God at His prom-ise

A   A7   D   A

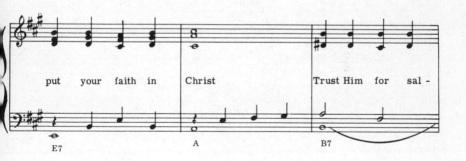

put   your   faith   in   Christ   Trust Him   for   sal -

E7   A   B7

D.S.al Fine

- va - tion   And   e - - ter - - nal   life!

E   E7

240 What a friend

Words: J.M. Scriven
Music: 'The carnival is over' by Tom Springfield

Slow 4 (with a beat)

What a friend_____ we have in Je - sus All our sins_____ and grief to bear!_____ What a priv - - - i-lege to car - ry Ev - 'ry -thing_____ to God in pray'r_____ O what peace_____ we of-ten

knows_____ our ev - 'ry weak - -ness: Take it

Bb   C7   F   Dm

1   2

to_____ the Lord in pray'r.   Are we pray'r._____

Bb   C7   F   C7   F

3. Are we weak and heavy-laden,
    Cumbered with a load of care?
    Jesus only is our refuge:
    Take it to the Lord in prayer.
    Do thy friends despise, forsake thee?
    Take it to the Lord in prayer;
    In His arms He'll take and shield thee!
    Thou wilt find a solace there.

4. What a friend we have in Jesus,
    All our sins and grief to bear!
    What a privilege to carry
    Everything to God in prayer.
    O what peace we often forfeit,
    O what needless pain we bear
    All because we do not carry
    Everything to God in prayer.

241 In the stillness

Words and Music: G. Brattle

Light and Rhythmic

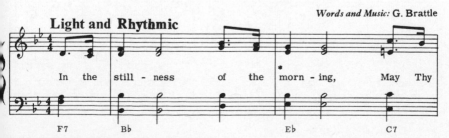

In   the   still - ness   of   the   morn - ing,   May Thy

F7   Bb   Eb   C7

* The word evening may be used when applicable.

voice a - lone be heard;——— In the quiet-ness of Thy

F7 Bb B F7 Bb

pres- ence May we hear God's liv - ing Word. In the one-ness of the

Eb C7 F7 Bb Eb

Spi - rit We would wait up - on Thee, Lord;——— In the

Bb C7 F7

still -ness of the morn-ing, May Thy blessing be out- poured.

Bb Eb G7 Cm C7 F F7 Bb

© G. Brattle 1969. By kind permission.

Dedication and Response

242 What He wants me

Words adapted and Music: N.L. Warren

2. Gracious Lord who died to save me,
   Bore my sins, in love forgave me,
   Life and joy and peace He gave me,
   For I am His own.
   Now my life belongs to Jesus,
   I am His and He is mine.

3. In His mercy Jesus needs me,
   With the light of Heaven He leads me,
   With the Bread of Life He feeds me,
   For I am His own.
   Now my life belongs to Jesus.
   I am His and He is mine.

© N.L. Warren 1969. By kind permission.

243 Now this is just the reason why

Words: from Romans 12. 1. J.H. Coulson
Music: J.G. Coulson

Now this is just the rea-son why I'm tell-ing you To pre--sent your - selves, give your lives to God To be a liv - ing sac - ri -fice that's ho - - - ly And ac--cep - ta - ble un - - - to Him.

Just think of all that His love has done for you, Just

think of all that His love has done for you, Just

think of all that His love could do still through you. So

So - this is just the reason why...

2. He sent His Son and He sent Him just for you,
   Who gave His life, and He gave it all for you
   Just think of all that His love would do yet for you.

And - that is just the reason why...

244 Don't let the world around

Words: from Romans 12. 2. J.H. Coulson
Music: J.G. Coulson (written primarily for the accordion)

Verse:

'Bow down, be like all the rest! ' So Daniel's friends were told. Daunt - less they faced the fi - nal test God brought them through that fire like gold.

Chorus:

Don't let the world a - round squeeze you in - to that
All through His Word it's told how God makes us

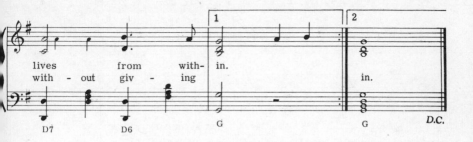

Single, David faced the giant,
Faith backed the stone he threw
Hear, too, Jonathan defiant -
'God saves by many or by few!'

Chorus

'Don't let the world around squeeze you into that same old mould,
Let God remould your lives from within.'
Why fight the fight alone, claim strength from God's own Son,
Whether by few or many He'll win.

Samson, though a mighty giant
And man of God it seems
Though called to serve the Lord his God
Falls before Delilah's schemes.

Chorus

'Don't let the world around squeeze you into that same old mould,
Let God remould your lives from within.'
Don't let them, friend or foe, draw you from the One you know,
Stay close to Jesus through thick or thin.

Joseph, just a slave to sell,
Gideon, poor farmer's boy,
Rebekah, working at the well -
For each fulfilment was God's plan.

Chorus

'Don't let the world around squeeze you into that same old mould,
Let God remould your lives from within.'
Obey His gracious Word, in everything make Him Lord,
Run the straight race with eyes fixed on Him.

245 If I tried

Words and Music: J. McKenzie
arr: N.L. Warren

1. If I tried to live_____ for You Lord, to-day,_____ If I tried to fol-low Your won-der-ful way, Then all of my life would be me and not You_____ And none of Your glo-ry would

ev - er shine | through.

A7   D   A7   D

you.____

A7   D   G   D

Melody for 2nd Verse begins:

Since I first met You,____ I knew, Lord, You were the way,

2. Since I first met You, I knew Lord You were the way,
   I tried hard to walk in Your footsteps each day,
   But somehow my life didn't glorify Thee,
   So make me a channel, and You live through me.

3. Take each new day, whatever's in store,
   Take my whole being and into me pour,
   Your power, and Your Spirit, Oh make me anew,
   For no-one can change me, Lord Jesus, but You.

246 Just as I am

Words: C. Elliott (1789-1871)
Music: P.M. Verrall

Lamb   of God,   I   come.

D7   G

2.   Just as I am, poor, wretched, blind, -
     Sight, riches, healing of the mind,
     Yea, all I need, in Thee to find,
     O Lamb of God, I come,

3.   Just as I am, Thou wilt receive,
     Wilt welcome, pardon, cleanse, relieve;
     Because Thy promise I believe,
     O Lamb of God, I come.

4.   Just as I am - Thy love unknown
     Has broken every barrier down -
     Now to be Thine, yea, Thine alone,
     O Lamb of God, I come.

5.   Just as I am, of that free love
     The breadth, length, depth and height to prove,
     Here for a season, then above, -
     O Lamb of God, I come.

247 Jesus grant that we may follow

Words: J. Young
Music: Traditional
arr: D.G. Wilson

Je - sus, grant that we may fol - low In our
Mas - ter, teach us how to fol - low On the

lives, the steps You trod; With Your life our in - spir -
road to Cal - va - ry. May Your mind be formed a -

- a - tion And our pat - tern, Son of God.

-mong us, From self - in - t'rest set us free.

2. Lord, we know we cannot follow
Till You save us from our sin.
May the fullness of Your Spirit
Give us risen power within.
Saviour, give us strength to follow
Your example and Your law;
Loving You above all others,
Others may we love the more.

3. Jesus, give us faith to follow
Through affliction, pain and toil.
In the dangerous times of plenty
Keep us faithful, true and loyal.
Peace in turmoil, strength in testing,
Patience in the slower hours;
Joy in life and love in all things,
These were Yours - Lord, make them ours.

Guidance

248   I know the Lord is leading me

Words: H. Kobler
tr: S. Lonsdale and M.A. Baughen
Music: H. Kobler

1. I know the Lord is lead - - ing me

me   He knows my path and

des - - ti - ny   In

ev - 'ry prob - lem   of   my   life_____   He

Dm7   Eb   Bb   Eb   F7

guides   me   I   know   the   Lord   is

C   D7   Gm

lead - - - ing   me._____

D7   Gm

2. It is the Saviour leading me
    Who rose from death triumphantly
    To whom all power in heaven and earth is given
    It is the Saviour leading me.

3. I trust my God in leading me
    Who said all things will work to be
    For good to those He calls, who love Him truly
    I trust my God in leading me.

249 The Lord is near you

Words and Music: N.L. Warren

The Lord is near___ you, right by your

side.   day.   The Lord is

near___ you,___ right by___ your side.___

2. The Lord will live in you, right in your heart.
His peace He'll give you, His love impart.
He will cleanse your sin away
He will teach you how to pray
When Jesus lives in you, right in your heart.

3. The Lord will come for you, at that Last Day,
When Heaven will open its shining way.
Will you be ready then?
Will you be trusting Him?
When Jesus comes again, at that Last Day.

The Lord is near you, right by your side.

250 Wherever He goes

Words and Music: A. Culverwell

Slowly, with very relaxed rhythm

1. I will fol-low where-ev-er He leads,
3. When the sun starts to set in the sky,

Ev-'ry prob-lem my Sav-iour He
I shall know that I'm near-er my

knows: though the path may be long with His
home: but un-til that great day I shall

help I'll be strong, I will go just where-ev-er He
still trust and pray, And I'll go just where-ev-er He

goes. ____
goes. ____ } 2.He may lead me to

coun-tries where trou-bles sur-round; ev-en

there He'll be with me, I know____ I prom-ise I'll
fol - low where - ev – er Christ leads me, and so I will

E7   A7
D   D7   G   D

D.C. al Fine

go   just where - ev – er He goes.____

D   A7   D

251 If you know the Lord

Words and Music: B. Reichner

head - in' home____ He'll show you the way.____

G7   cresc.   C7

___ If you know the Lord,_____ You need no-

F   F7

-bo - dy else____ to see the light,_____ His won-der-ful

Bb   Bb6   F   C7

1. light,_____ If you know the
2. light.

F   —C7   F   Bb6 Bbm   F

252 My Lord's in charge of my life

Words and Music: R. Germain

2. I put my life in His hands, His hands,
    I put my life in His hands
    A slave to Him I am fully free
    I put my life in His hands.

3. He's got a wonderful plan, for me,
    He's got a wonderful plan
    My future's safe though I cannot see
    For He's got a wonderful plan.

4. I'll trust my wonderful Lord, my Lord,
    I'll trust my wonderful Lord
    He cannot fail and He cares for me
    I'll trust my wonderful Lord.

Christian Living

253 The happy people

Words and Music: C. Blissard-Barnes

Hap-py, those,———— who know they're poor, For the King-—dom now is theirs, Hap-py, those——whose grief is sore,———— For God will wipe a-way their tears.

2. Happy, those who are the meek,
   They'll inherit all the earth;
   Happy, those who truly seek
   And hunger for His righteousness and worth.

3. For the Saviour whom they know,
   Always satisfies their heart;
   Happy those who mercy show,
   For they'll obtain God's mercy for their part.

4. Happy, you, the pure in heart,
   You will see God in His Heaven;
   Happy, too, the folk whose lot
   It is to bring true peace to men.

5. This great blessing shall be theirs,
   In the glory soon to come;
   They shall all be called God's heirs,
   When God the Father calls us to His Home.

6. Happy, now, you are when men
   Speak against you for my cause;
   You shall have a place in heaven,
   And great reward shall then be yours.

254 It's not an easy road

Words: J. W. Peterson
Music: S. Beckley
arr. D. G. Wilson

No no it's not an ea-sy road No
No it's not an ea-sy road; But Je-sus walks beside me and
brightens the journey, and lightens ev-'ry hea-vy load.

2. It's not an easy road, there are trials and troubles,
    And many are the dangers we meet;
    But Jesus guards and keeps so that nothing can harm us,
    And smooths the rugged path for our feet.
        Chorus

3. Though I am often footsore and weary from travel,
    Though I am often bowed down with care;
    A better day is coming when home in the glory,
    I'll rest in perfect peace over there.
        Chorus

255 The heavenly way

Words and Music: B.J. Stephenson

While trav-el-ling on the heav'n - - ly way I

know I'll al-ways need God's prec-ious Word, which

is my sword, And prayer which is my shield. My

Sav-iour's pres-ence keeps and guides Through

-out each pass - ing day I'll nev-er fear the

C6 G C6

path - - way A - long that heav'n- ly way.

G Am7 D7 G

2. He's always there beside me
On every mountain side
All thoughts of stumbling flee from me
With Jesus as my guide.
For every footstep that I take
I know He took before
My only wish along the way
Is that I'll know Him more.

3. I read my Bible on the way
To keep me on the road
For if I falter either way
Many snares abound.
I keep in touch with Him by prayer
To keep me free from sin.
I long for that tremendous day
When I can be with Him.

4. For at the end of this same road
There is a place, He said,
Prepared for those who trust in Him
Risen from the dead.
'Worthy the Lamb' my lips will cry
When I before Him come
For ever in His family
When I arrive at home.

256 My sheep hear my voice

Music: J. Van Den Hogen
arr: D.G. Wilson

257 Invisible chains

Words: P. Monk
Music: M.A. Baughen
arr: M.C.T. Strover

2.   God's power is visible,
        And God's power is real -
        The power of love stronger than steel;
            Stronger than steel
            - Can't you see? -
            Power of Love
            Sets me free.

        Invisible chains, holding me fast,
        - And now, my Lord, is my bondage past?

3.   God's chains are invisible,
        God's chains are real -
        Chains of love stronger than steel:
            Stronger than steel
            - You can see -
            Chains of Love
            Holding me free.

        Invisible chains, holding me fast
        - Forever, Lord, may this freedom last!

258   Each new day, Lord

Words and Music: M.G. Schneider
tr: S. Lonsdale and M.A. Baughen

Each new day, Lord,

F   Fmaj.7

I give it back in-to Your hands for You gave it to me

Dm7   Gm7 C7   F   Fmaj.7 Dm Bb6 C7 F6

You, my Lord, are   the source of time and of its end - ing, I   am

F   Fmaj.7   Dm7   Gm7 C7   F   Bb Fmaj.7 Dm

You make darkness light. Each new day, Lord, I give it back in-to Your

Dm Cm7 F Cm F Fmaj.9 Fmaj.7 Dm7 Gm7 C7

hands for You gave it to me You, my Lord, are

F Bb Fmaj.7 Dm Bb6 C7 Bb F Fmaj.7

the source of time and of its end - ing, I am

Dm7   Gm7 C7   F   Bb   Fmaj.7   Dm

trust-ing You.

Bb6 C7 Bb   F

I am trust - ing You.

Fmaj. Dm Bb C7 Bb   F

2. When a day is finished and I look back
    I have often failed you - with sins that are black
    Yet You cleanse me, O Lord.
         Chorus

3. Many words would have been - better unsaid
    Hardly any thanking - but grumbling instead
    Lord You know what I'm like.
         Chorus

4. Life is all so pointless, lived without You,
    Yet You give it purpose when you're leading me.
    My path you know, O Lord.
         Chorus

259 Please don't ever let me look back

Words and Music: C. Burns
arr. D.G. Wilson

1 & 4. Dark was my night with-out you Lord.
2. Long were those years of my blind - - - ness

F   Am   Cm   D

Long was that nev - er end-ing track.
Strong were those chains a - cross my back.

Gm   F

Thank You for find-ing me. Thank You for guiding me. But
Thank You for sav-ing me. Thank You for lov-ing me. But

Bb   F   Dm

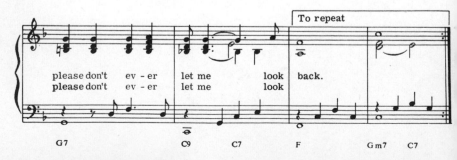

To repeat

please don't ev - er let me look back.
please don't ev - er let me look

G7   C9   C7   F   Gm7   C7

D.C.

guide me   as I   work   and as I   rest.

Gm9   C7   G9   C9

260 We shall overcome

Words and Music: Traditional
arr: D.G. Wilson

We   shall   ov - er - come,____   We   shall   ov - er -

-come,_____   We   shall   ov - er - come   some

C   F   G   Am7   D7

day;_____   By   faith   in

G   D7   G   G7   Am   Em   F

Christ   I   do   be - lieve

C   F   G6   G7   Am

We   shall   ov - er - come   some   day.

C   F   Dm   C   G7   C

In verses 2 & 3, lines 1, 2 & 3 begin on the last crotchet of the preceding bar:-

The   truth will   make   us   etc.

2.   The truth will make us free,
      The truth will make us free,
      The truth will make us free some day;
      By faith in Christ I do believe
      We shall overcome some day.

3.   The Lord will see us through,
      The Lord will see us through,
      The Lord will see us through some day.
      By faith in Christ I do believe
      We shall overcome some day.

4.   We shall live in peace,
      We shall live in peace,
      We shall live in peace some day;
      By faith in Christ I do believe
      We shall overcome some day.

5.   We shall overcome
      We shall overcome,
      We shall overcome some day,
      By faith in Christ I do believe
      We shall overcome some day.

O

Testimony

261 The answer

Words: D. J. Jackman
Music: G. Arlidge

262 You need Him too

Words and Music: J.K. Davies and B.J. Heather

I was a sin-ner lone-ly and sad,

Je-sus came to me and He made me glad,

Now He has found me His peace does sur-round me

2. The peace that He gave me was bought on a cross,
He brought me salvation from suffering and loss
He died to save me, His own life He gave me
You need Him too, oh yes; you need Him too, oh yes;
You need Him too.

3. He gives me power to overcome sin,
He gives me His peace and victory within,
My Saviour protects me, His purpose directs me
You need Him too, oh yes; you need Him too, oh yes;
You need Him too.

263 If you ask me

Words and Music: N.L. Warren

If you ask me, how I know that Je-sus Christ is

F   Dm7   Gm7   C7   F   F7

real,_____ I'll tell you that I trust His Word And

Bb   D7   Gm   C7   F   Dm

not just what I feel. He came to me, He

F   Bb   F   F7   Bb   F6

lives in me, He fills my heart with love._____ I

Gm   Eb   Cm   F7   Bb   D7

know Him as my Liv- ing Friend Who leads me on to

Gm   C7   F   Dm   F   Bb

1 & 2   **3**

heav'n a - - bove.   -bove.   Who

Gm   C7   F   F

leads me on to heav'n a - - bove.

Bb   Gm   C7   F

2. If you ask me, how I know
   My sins are all forgiven,
   I'll tell you how my Saviour died
   To pave my way to Heaven.
      He suffered there in lonely pain,
      Cut off from God for me.
      He took the burden of my guilt,
      He died alone to set me free.

3. If you ask me, how I know
   There's life beyond the grave,
   I'll tell you, Jesus rose again,
   Victorious to save.
      He came to me, He lives in me,
      He fills my heart with love.
      I know Him as my living Friend
      Who leads me on to Heaven above,
      Who leads me on to Heaven above.

264 Surely goodness and mercy

Words and Music: John W. Peterson and A.B.S.

Smoothly, in a steady tempo

1. A pil-grim was I, and a-wan-d'ring,

In the cold night of sin I did roam,

When Je-sus the kind Shep-herd found me,

And now I am on my way home.

Sure - ly good - ness and mer - cy shall fol - - low

Eb

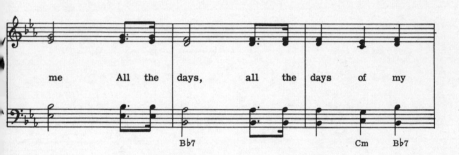

me All the days, all the days of my

Bb7 Cm Bb7

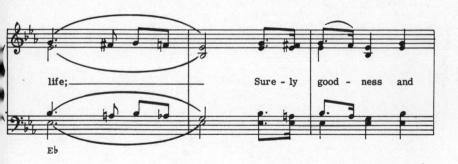

life; _____ Sure - ly good - ness and

Eb

mer - cy shall fol - - - low me All the

mer - cy shall fol - low me All the

Eb

D.C.

days, all the days of my life._____

Bb7   Eb

CODA (after last chorus only)

p **Slowly**

All the days, all the days of my life._____

Bb7   Eb

2. He restoreth my soul when I'm weary,
    He giveth me strength day by day;
    He leads me beside the still waters,
    He guards me each step of the way.
        Chorus

3. When I walk thru the dark lonesome valley,
    My Saviour will walk with me there;
    And safely His great hand will lead me
    To the mansions He's gone to prepare.
        Chorus

265 O happy day

Words: P. Doddridge
Music: T.R. Jones

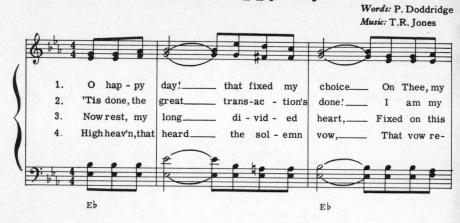

1. O hap-py day! that fixed my choice On Thee, my
2. 'Tis done, the great trans-ac-tion's done! I am my
3. Now rest, my long di-vid-ed heart, Fixed on this
4. High heav'n, that heard the sol-emn vow, That vow re-

Eb   Eb

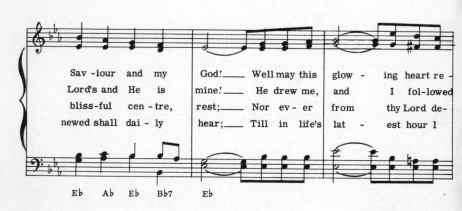

Sav-iour and my God! Well may this glow-ing heart re-
Lord's and He is mine! He drew me, and I fol-lowed
bliss-ful cen-tre, rest; Nor ev-er from thy Lord de-
newed shall dai-ly hear; Till in life's lat-est hour I

Eb Ab Eb Bb7   Eb

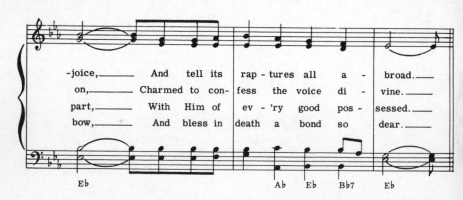

-joice, And tell its rap-tures all a-broad.
on, Charmed to con-fess the voice di-vine.
part, With Him of ev-'ry good pos-sessed.
bow, And bless in death a bond so dear.

Eb   Ab Eb Bb7   Eb

266 My Lord is real

Words and Music: N.T. Faithfull
arr: D.G. Wilson

(last time repeat 2nd half)

2. Trust and believe is what you must do,
And His spirit will come unto you
Guide you in His perfect way
Till He comes again one day.

3. The Lord will judge us when He comes
And we'll stand righteous in the Son
No condemnation now we fear
With Jesus ever near

No condemnation now we fear
With Jesus ever near.

267 For me to live is Christ

Words and Music: J. White
arr: N.L. Warren

Music for
Chorus and Verse:

Chorus
words: For me to live is Christ, to die is gain,____
(start with chorus)

(v4) ____ To hold His hand, and walk His nar-row way.

There is no peace, no joy, no thrill, Like walk-ing in His
1. When He
2. He who

will, For me to live is Christ, to die is gain.____

1. Now once my heart was full of sin and shame
    Till someone told me Jesus came to save,
    When He said 'Come home to me',
    He set my poor heart free
    For me to live is Christ, to die is gain.
      Chorus

2. Now there are things that I still do not know
    But of this one thing I'm completely sure.
    He who called me on that day,
    Washed all my sin away,
    For me to live is Christ, to die is gain.
      Chorus

P

268 I've got a song in my heart

Words and Music: G. McClelland
arr. P. Bye

I've got a   song in my heart._____   A mel - o - dy, And it's been

C   Am   Dm   G7

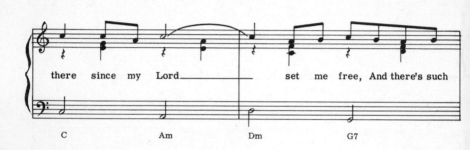

there since my Lord_____   set me free, And there's such

C   Am   Dm   G7

peace   in my heart_____   That I can scarce be - lieve it's

C   Am   Dm   G7

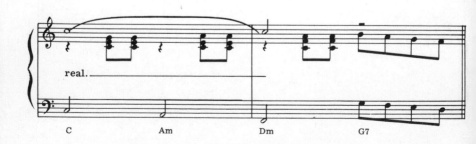

real._____

C   Am   Dm   G7

Joy in my life.___ I want to tell you There's no

C   Am   Dm   G7

strug - gle, no strife___ And it was Christ a- bove a -

C   Am   Dm   G7

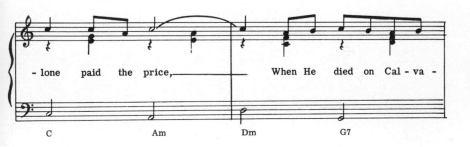

- lone paid the price,___ When He died on Cal - va -

C   Am   Dm   G7

-ry.___

C   F   C

269 My story so sad

Words and Music: A.R. Bell

1. My sto - ry so sad,_____ Wand- 'rin' down life's emp - ty _____ road,_____ Hav - ing such a hea -vy load to bear,_____ Did- n't know someone was there, Wait-ing for me._____ I'd gone my way,_____ Tried to find what hap-pi-ness I could,_____

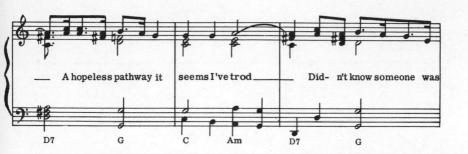

A hopeless pathway it seems I've trod___ Did-n't know someone was

Chorus:(after vv. 1 & 2)

there, Wait-ing for me. Man-y years

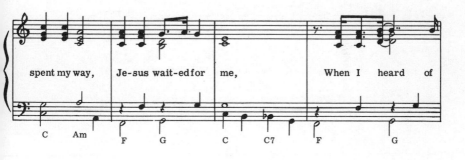

spent my way, Je-sus wait-ed for me, When I heard of

new life in Him, I found the meaning of Cal - va - ry.

Verses 2 and 3

2. Now He's mine,_____ Sav-iour and my King,__ Lord of all,

3. Now I sing_____ of sal - va -tion's plan, How it's free,__

C   Am   D7   G7   C   Am

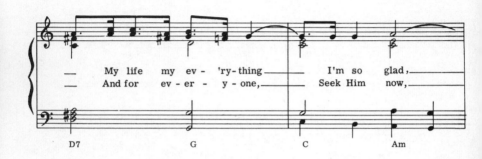

__ My life my ev - 'ry-thing_____ I'm so glad,__

__ And for ev - er - y - one,_____ Seek Him now,__

D7   G   C   Am

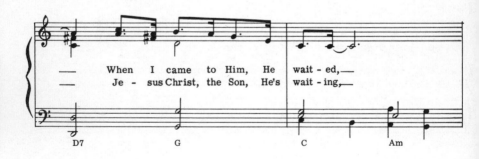

__ When I came to Him, He wait - ed,__

__ Je - sus Christ, the Son, He's wait - ing,__

D7   G   C   Am

Coda after verse 3.

Fine

wait -ed for me.(to chos.)   He's wait-ing for you.

wait-ing for you.(to coda)

F   G   F   G7   C

Outreach
270 Hustle Bustle

Words and Music: R.G. Wright and K. Lamming

2. Got to keep up with the Jones,
   Things are so important!
   Spending money, getting loans,
   Where d'you think you're going to?

3. What are your priorities?
   Who d'you really want to please?
   Living in this world today,
   People seem to lose their way, Oh!

4. Jesus said 'I am the Way',
   Won't you listen to Him?
   For His words apply today
   Where d'you think you're going to?

5. If you really put Him first,
   Take Him as your Lord and guide,
   He will give you life that's real
   Life that springs afresh inside, Oh!

6. Jesus said 'I am the Way',
   Won't you listen to Him?
   For His words apply today
   Where d'you think you're going to?

271 Time

Words and Music: The Crossbeats

1. Won't you stop and think a-bout the life you're tast -ing? Are you really worried 'bout the time you're wast-ing? Well, we've come to tell you now Yes, we've come to tell you how, How you can re- deem the time____

-deem the time_____ that you have lost.   Well

Bb   A7   D   F#7

we a-gree   there's a time   for   liv-ing;   But

B   B7   E

can't you see,   now's the time   to give in?   We

A   A7   D   F#

see the time   and it's go-ing   by each day,   And there'll

B   B7   E

come a time when it's all gone a-way. gone a-way.

A   A7   D   D

3. It was sometime in the past Jesus spent His time,
   When the skies were overcast, paying for your crime
   And we've come to tell you now,
   Yes, we've come to tell you how,
   How you can redeem the time that you have lost.
   Chorus

© Sky Sounds. By kind permission.

272 Crazy mixed up generation

Words and Music: The Crossbeats
arr: J. and B. Courtie

Let's face it friends, the world is in— such a mess!

E   A   E   B7

Be - fore life ends, let's start liv-ing!

E   A   B7

234

lost, but what's the an-swer?

Chorus:

Cra-zy,mixed-up

A   B7   Dm

gen-er-a-tion, there is on-ly one sol-u-tion Je-sus is the

G   C   Am   Dm

great sen-sa-tion! Won't you stop and think, Now you're on the

G   F#m   B7   F#m

Final additional chorus only.

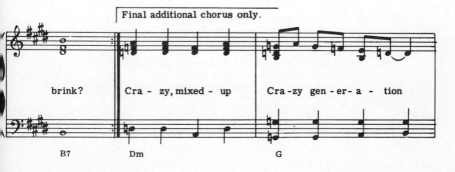

brink? Cra-zy,mixed-up Cra-zy gen-er-a-tion

B7   Dm   G

there is   on-ly   one   sol - u - tion;   Je - sus   is   the

C   Am   Dm

great   sen- sa- tion!   Won't you stop and   think,   Now you're on the

G   F#m   B7   F#m

brink?

B7   F#m   B7   E

2. Beats think life's a joke, these long-haired cynics of society;
    They don't do a stroke... but why should they?
    Mum and Dad at home have lost control of their pride and joy;
    Oh, how they moan! What's the answer?
        Chorus

3. Can you be so blind? You can't see the truth about yourself!
    Or don't you mind where you're going?
    Jesus knows it all. He knows your situation now.
    Why do you stall when He's the answer?
        Chorus

273 He waits

Words and Music: The Crossbeats
arr: J. and B. Courtie

1. There is some-one wait-ing, And He waits so pa-tient-ly To be your friend and take a-way your sin.

He waits con-tin-ual-ly, So pa-tient-ly, He's wait-ing; Oh won't you come to Him?

Chorus:

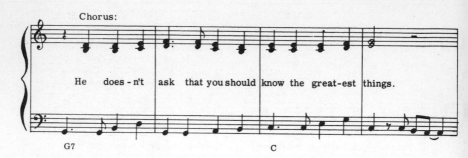

He does-n't ask that you should know the great-est things.

G7   C

So come to Him and don't de - lay.

G7   C   C7

Come to Him as you are;   Re-mem-ber He's not far a-

F   B7

-way from you,   He's not far a - way   from you.

C   F   C   G7

you.

G7   C   F   Fm6   C   C6

2. Why keep Jesus waiting? Don't you know that He loves you?
   And He's the answer to your emptiness, my friend.
   He waits continually, so patiently,
   Will you say yes? It's worth it in the end!
   Chorus

274 The shores of Galilee

Words and Music: C. Burns
arr. A.H. Ramell

Verses 1, 2 & 5

1. See the snow_____ drift-ing o'er the mea-dows;

Dm   Gm   F   A7   Dm

Gen-tle death_____ from the dis-mal grey skies_____

Gm   C

Q

Sum-mer's gone,_____ Mother Nat-ure's weeping,_____

Gm   F   A7   Dm

To repeat

And her tears_____ turn to ice in her eyes.

Gm   F   D7   Gm

To continue   Verses 3, 4 & 6

soul. 3.Last night   I dreamed I was in   Ga-li-lee._____

Gm   G   D   Am7   D

_____ A - lone   I watched for hours that sil - ent sea._____

Am7   D   Am7   D

A fisherman's net of twine was ly-ing in the sand. The one that Si - mon Pe-ter left, to take his Sav-iour's hand. own.

Am7   D maj.7   D7   G9   Em   A7   D maj.7   D7   G9   Em   A7   D   D

2. Man can run from the cold of winter;
   Build a fire with a handful of coal.
   But the blaze of a thousand pine trees,
   Never melts all the ice in his soul.

4. Last night, I roamed the shores of Galilee
   That net, forgotten there, made sense to me.
   Peter turned his back on all he'd ever known
   To follow one who knew the Way, to make that life his own.

5. When the cold seems to be so endless
   Grows a flower, small and weak but alive.
   Spring is here, and the ice is melting.
   'It is finished!' cried the Lord as He died.

6. Last night, I roamed the shores of Galilee
   That net, forgotten there, made sense to me.
   Peter turned his back on all he'd ever known
   To follow one who knew the Way, to make that life his own.

275 Long and lonely journey

Words and Music: C. Burns
arr: D.G. Wilson

It's a long, long, long and lone-ly jour-ney_____ It's a

long, long, long and lone-ly road. You need

help to light-en your bur-den, You need

help to car-ry that load. So give your life to the

Lord. Give your life to the Lord. And you'll

F#m7   B7   E   C#m   F#m7   B7

know how it feels,— To be loved as you

Bm7   C#7   F#m

go. On that glor - ious ev - er-last - ing

Am7   E   B7

jour - ney. On that glor - ious, nev - er end-ing road.

C#m   F#m7   E   B9   E

© C. Burns and D.G. Wilson 1969. By kind permission.

276 Your fancy clothes

Words and Music: G. McClelland
arr: P. Bye

1. Your fan-cy clothes, the way you wear your hair_ You cher-ish those, You say you real-ly care_ But when the moth and

2. You buy a car, you keep it shining bright.
On your guitar, the label is just right.
But when the night and fear come,
And you feel a tear come,
You'll want a friend, there won't be one in sight.

3. You're smiling now, but round the corner's pain.
You wonder how, you'll ever laugh again.
Then you'll remember, slowly,
The things that I told you
About my Lord, and all that He has said.

277 Listen to the story

Words and Music: G. McClelland
arr: P. Bye

A   E7

Lis-ten to the sto-ry

A   E7   A

Of the lit-tle can-dle, Just a lit-tle sto-ry

E7   A

but the tale is am-ple Lets you know what I mean

E7   A   A7

may-be too what you mean When we talk of liv-ing and of

1 & 2 | 3 | 4

liv-ing to the full___ way a-round. sto - - - -ry.

D   Dm   A   B7

B7   E7   B7   E7   E7   A

2. Stands the little candle in a darken'd window,
   Tho' it has potential by itself it won't glow
   Till a lighted taper gently shines upon it,
   Touches it and passes on the light which it has on it.

3. Now that little candle lights the darken'd window,
   Shines for people outside, glows on people in too
   Just a tiny candle with its little glimmer,
   Yet the light is seen for quite a way around.

4. We are just like candles, someone needs to light us,
   We have the potential, someone needs to guide us:
   Jesus light our darkness, use us for your glory,
   Shining as the candle in the story.

278 We must believe

Words and Music: D. Lowe
arr. N.L. Warren

Down from His glo - ry the Sav-iour came, In - to a world of sin and shame,

Seek-ing men to love His Fa - ther's name,_____ "Come un - to me" He is our Sav-iour, our guide and friend_____

He is the one on whom we can de-pend, He is our on-ly hope,

G   A   A7   D   D7

world with-out end,_____ We must be - lieve.

G   Gm6   D   A7   D

2.   Jesus, the perfect one was humble and kind,
     Healing the halt, the lame and the blind -
     Such power could conquer sin, renew the mind,
     'Follow thou me'.
     Chorus

3.   Rich, yet for our sakes he became poor,
     He's our example for evermore.
     God's love in all of us means peace not war,
     'Abide in me'.
     Chorus

4.   If we are Christ's, and take the Spirit's sword,
     One day we shall see our blessed Lord,
     What exultation in that glad reward,
     'Rejoice with me'.
     Chorus

5.   Learning to live with Christ on this earth below,
     Finding a purpose the world cannot know,
     Looking to Jesus till our lives o'erflow
     'With charity'.
     Chorus

279 Think again

Words: V. Hadert
Music: Cliff Richard
arr. M.C.T. Strover

If___ ac-cess to hea-ven de-pen-ded on you, On the

num-ber of good deeds you'd done; What a

won-der-ful pic-ture you'd paint of your-self- I'm quite

sure you'd rate sec-ond to none.

2. But God's not concerned with the things you've achieved,
   Though these things may be many or few;
   There's only one way by which men may reach God,
   And that doesn't mean all men but you.

3. Jesus said I'm the Way and the Truth and the Life,
   No man cometh to God but by Me;
   And that way back to God is to trust in the Blood
   That was shed for you - at Calvary.

4. It is Christ's Blood alone that has power to cleanse
   From the dire consequences of sin;
   And it's only on seeing that sin-cleansing Blood
   That the Father will say 'Enter in'; 'Enter in'.

5. All have sinned and fall short of the glory of God,
   And the Bible has made it quite plain -
   That your righteousnesses are to Him filthy rags
   If you think they'll avail, Think again.

280 Have you ever wished

Words and Music: C. Burns
arr. D.G. Wilson

Have you ev-er wished you knew how to pray?
Do you ev-er won - der why you're a - live?

F   Dm

Have you ev-er wished you knew what to say?
Do you ev-er wish you knew?

Gm7   C7   C7

I know you do. I've found the an-swer for a

F   F   Dm

lone- ly emp-ty heart; Take Je - sus in your life and

Gm7   C7   F   Dm

make an - oth - er start.   Oh,

Gm7   C7   Bb

D C al Fine

peo - ple!   Lis - ten all you peo - ple!

F   Gm7   C7

2   I've found the answer for a lonely empty soul;
    Take Jesus in your life and He will make you whole.
    Oh, people! Listen all you people!

    Anybody saved can learn how to pray
    Anybody saved can know what to say
    Anybody saved knows why he's alive
    Do you ever wish you knew?
    I know you do.

281 Simply believe

Words and Music: A. Winkworth

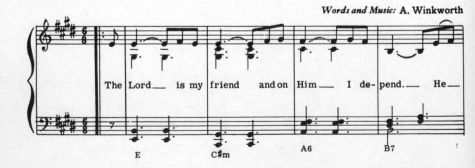

The Lord___ is my friend   and on Him___ I de - pend.   He___

E   C#m   A6   B7

guides us— on our way   and for - ev - er with us will   stay,— If we

E   C#m   F#m   B7

trust,— trust in   Him,— He will   lead   us   ev - 'ry - -

E   C#m   F#m   B7

day   He will   lead   us

E   C#m   F#m7

Interlude

ev - - - - er - y   day.

B7   E   C#m   A   B7

2. One thing is required that we trust in our God.
   For He died on the tree to set us all free
   From the bond of our sin, just simply believe in Him.

3. Come now to the cross with your faith small and weak,
   He will help you to believe if only Him you'll seek.
   He will come in to your heart and He'll reign in every part.

4. The Lord is my friend and on Him I depend.
   He guides us on our way and forever with us will stay,
   If we trust, trust in Him, He will lead us every day.

R

282 His name is Jesus

Steady tempo

Words and Music: D. Drinkall

I have got a friend that's true   Someone who will

see me through,   He guides me in all I do

—— His Name is   Je - sus.   When I stum - ble

He is there,   all my trou-bles He will share

He's the Sav - iour, the One who cares His Name is
Je - sus. How ev - er great the storm He will
make the wa - ters calm, And through the dark-est
night Je - sus is the guid-ing light.

I find com-fort when I read of the things He's

done for me Yes, I've got a Friend in - deed

His Name is Je - sus His Name is Je - sus.

2. When the road seems hard and long and things keep on going wrong,
   Someone always makes me strong, His Name is Jesus.
   Sometimes on life's restless waves I'm a ship without a sail.
   But my Captain will never fail, His Name is Jesus.
   The joy that He imparts brings a warmness to my heart
   That's far beyond compare to the earthly joys I share!
   While I walk and talk with Him all my battles He will win,
   He helps me in everything, His Name is Jesus, His Name is Jesus.

3. Friends around me, young and old, don't be orphans in the cold,
   Come to One who loves you so, His Name is Jesus.
   Earthly treasures you possess won't give deep down happiness,
   Only One ever will do that, His Name is Jesus.
   This modern world today soon can lead your heart astray,
   There's so much sin and strife creeping into every life.
   Yet there's one sure way you can overcome the Devil's plan.
   Put your faith and trust in One, His Name is Jesus, His Name is Jesus.

283 My friend Joe

Words and Music: **G. Arlidge**

Joe's my friend and he thought I was mad, And he used to work so hard, in the of-fice near the yard, He was work-ing nine 'til five, Think-ing mon-ey all the time, And now he knows

knows   he   was wrong, And now   he   knows,

F7   Bb   Eb   Ab

knows   he   was wrong, And now   he   knows.

F7   Bb   Eb

Chorus

Je - sus says "I   am   the Way, the   Truth and the   Life   And with

Cm   G7   Cm   G7

me   will   you   on - ly   find   light".   (After verses 1 & 2)   He
                                                    (After verse 3)   He
                                                    (After verse 4)   He

Bb   F   C sus.F   C

died for me; I died with Him and so my life has changed And my
died for Joe; he died with Him and so his life has changed And his
died for you; please die with Him and then your life will change And your

world will nev-er be the same.
world can nev-er be the same.
world will nev-er be the

same.   And your world will nev-er be the same.

2. Joe then thought, "Now I'll work for the poor",
    And he used to give his time to the people who were blind,
    And he was searching for some point to give purpose to his life,
    And now he knows, that's not enough......
        Chorus

3. Then one day when his mood was so sad,
    For he'd given up all hope and his footsteps were so slow,
    But then he saw a smiling man who placed a booklet in his hand
    It was the Word, Word of the Lord......
        Chorus

4. Yes, he's changed quite beyond all belief,
    And he likes to work so hard, in the office near the yard,
    And he's found a new life now, thinks the world of the Lord,
    Because he knows, knows what is life.
    Because he knows the Lord is living in him..... And now he knows......
        Chorus

284   Does His claim ring true

Words and Music: R.G. Wright
arr. D.G. Wilson

Long   a - go,   when
Said   His   Fa - - - - - -ther

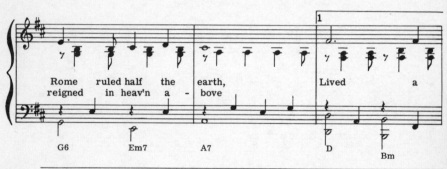

Rome   ruled half   the   earth,   Lived   a
reigned   in heav'n a -   bove

man   who   came   of   hum - ble   birth.   He

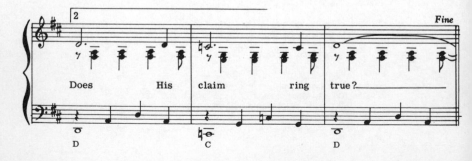

Does   His   claim   ring   true?

After verse 2 & 3 only.

2. Hear   this   might - - - y

D7   G

Jew,   Does   His

D
Bm   B7

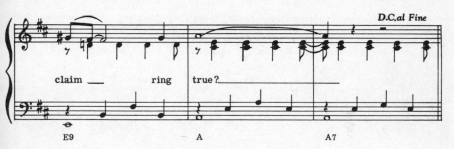

D.C. al Fine

claim ___   ring   true?___

E9   A   A7

2.   Crowds would follow everywhere He went
     And He told them why He had been sent
     To save the world through God's redeeming love
     Does His claim ring true?
       Hear this mighty Jew
       Does His claim ring true?

3.   Was He just a man who'd lost His mind
     Was He just a fraud, yet you will find
     That He healed the sick and cured the blind
     Does His claim ring true?
       Hear Him for He said
       I will rise from the dead.

4.   Was He just a man who'd lost His mind
     Was He just a fraud, yet you will find
     That His Church was born because it knew
     That His claim rings true.

285 Are you going my way

Words and Music: V. Howard and P. Howard
arr. N.L. Warren

Rhythm fairly free

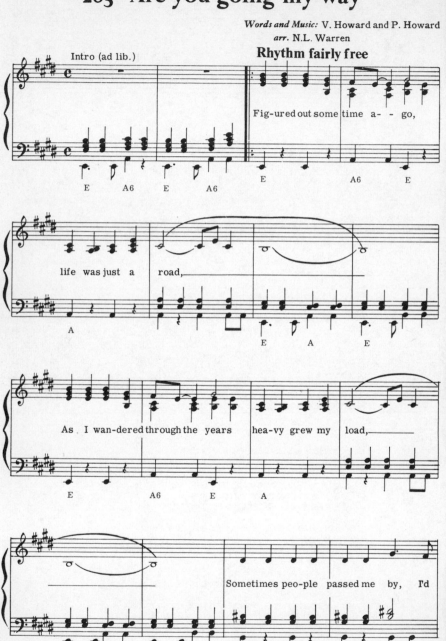

Fig-ured out some time a- - go, life was just a road,___ As I wan-dered through the years hea-vy grew my load,___ Sometimes peo-ple passed me by, I'd

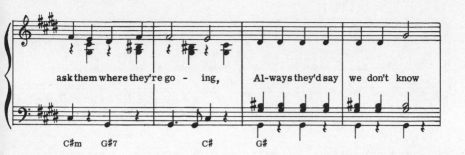

ask them where they're go - ing,   Al-ways they'd say we don't know

C#m   G#7   C#   G#

Our wild oats we've got to sow,   Don't ask questions just you keep on

C#m   Am   Am6

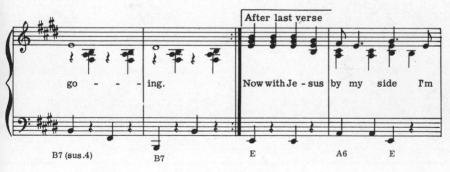

go - - -ing.   Now with Je - sus by my side   I'm

B7 (sus.4)   B7   E   A6   E

After last verse

on the oth - er high - - - way,

A   E   A6   E

Now I call to all my friends, Are you go-ing my____

E   A6   E   A

Same speed

way?____   Are____   you   go - -

E   A   Am

- - -ing   my   way?____

E   E6   E

2. So I journeyed down the road,
   The only one I'm knowing,
   Soon my burdens and my cares
   On me began a-showing,
   In despair to God I cried,
   Please hear what I am saying,
   Can't you show me some way out,
   Though I haven't any doubt
   I just didn't know what I was saying.

3. Then one day I saw a man,
   On another highway,
   Called to me across the stream,
   Are you going my way?
   I said thanks I don't think so,
   Why should I change direction,
   He said listen change your mind,
   Can't you see that corner's blind
   Please don't wait too long
   Before correction.

4. I said Okay, what's your name,
   He told me it was Jesus,
   Told me that the road I'm on
   The devil made to keep us,
   Reaching out across the stream
   He said you'll have to trust me,
   As I reached His outstretched hand
   I suddenly could understand
   This could be no ordinary man.

   Now with Jesus by my side,
   I'm on the other highway,
   Now I call to all my friends,
   Are you going my way.
   Are you going my way.

286 Reflections

Words: K. Craddock
Music: Cliff Richard
arr. M.C.T. Strover

One night I had a dream, through a swirling fog I walked a-lone by the edge of a stream I heard somebody groan, I stopped and

feet   shoes of   pain,   the   coat was   strife   the

chain was pride   I   saw   the re-flection   and I cried,   I

A   G

F#   Bm   A   G   F#

saw   the re-flec-tion,   and I   cried,_____

Bm   A   G   F#   Bm

Tears for myself a fool,   a man chained by inde-pen-dence

G#m   Bm

saw the re-flec-tion, chang-ing now. A

Bm   A   G   F#7

Slower

man was in my place, a man with holes in his hands and side, A

Bm

man I could not face,— the man I had cru-ci-fied,— on

A

him was my coat, my chains and my shoes, and be-

G   F#

287 A boy once sat

Words and Music: G. McClelland
arr: P. Bye

Intro:

Cm   Bb   Ab   G7   Cm   Bb   Ab   G7

A boy once sat by the side of a riv-er Dip-ping his feet in the

Cm   Fm   Cm   Eb

cool, cool, wa-ter, He watched the lit-tle fish-es a - laz-il-y swim-ming

G7   Cm   Fm   G7

by. _____ He looked up in - to the

Cm   Bb   Ab   G7   Cm

3   *Fine*

He'd —

Ab   G7   Cm   Bb   Cm   Bb Cm

(Vocal part vv 2 & 3)

heard a-bout a book and they called it the Bi-ble, and some folks said it was

on - ly a fa - ble, But no - one else could tell him how to

live or what would hap - pen when he died._____ So he

read, at the start ev - 'ry - thing had been per - fect, But

chan - ges had come through a man's dis - o - bed - ience, But

God still loved him so He sent His Son to suf - fer and____

die._____ And he mar-velled at a God who loved the

birds and the fish-es And yet sent His on - ly lov - ing

Son to suf-fer and to die.___ What could he do now to

gain God's af - fec - tion?___ How could his life___ take a

brand new di - rec - tion? He won-dered in his heart just ex -

- act - ly where the ans-wer did___ lie._____ So he

got down on his knees and he asked for for - giv-ness___ And

when he'd con - fessed, well, he want - ed to wit - ness He

shout-ed to the fish-es in the stream and the bird-ies in the sky___

___ And Christ was the ans-wer to the who, and the where and the

what, and the how, and the ans-wer_ to the why._____

288 The Bible tells me so

Words and Music: Traditional
arr: D.G. Wilson

1. There's a time to reap, a time to sow, That
2. There's a time to laugh, a time to cry, A

F   F maj.7

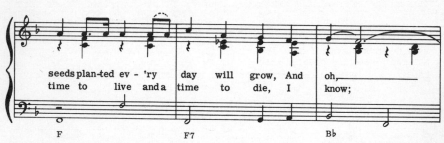

seeds plan-ted ev - 'ry day will grow, And oh,
time to live and a time to die, I know;

F   F7   Bb

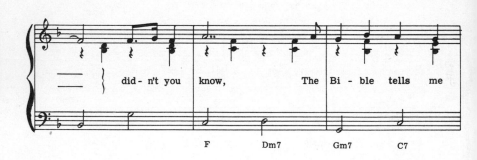

did - n't you know, The Bi - ble tells me

F   Dm7   Gm7   C7

Fine

so.   3. The good Lord watch-es ov - er ev - 'ry-one,

F   Bbm6

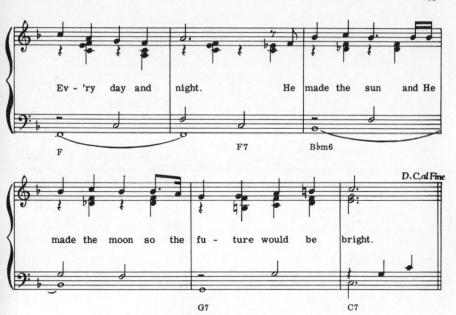

Ev - 'ry day and night. He made the sun and He

made the moon so the fu - ture would be bright.

D.C. al Fine

F   F7   Bbm6

G7   C7

4. There's a time to reap, a time to sow,
   A time to pray when the evening lights
   Are low, didn't you know,
   The Bible tells me so.

© in this arrangement only, D.G. Wilson 1969. By kind permission.

289 Think of tomorrow

Words and Music: C. Burns
arr. A.H. Ramell

CHORUS

Think of to-mor-row, what will it bring you? How can you face it

Bb   Eb   F   Bb

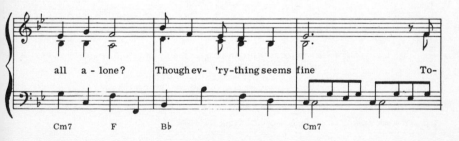

all a - lone? Though ev- 'ry-thing seems fine   To-

Cm7   F   Bb   Cm7

-mor-row is a long, long, time.

Cm7   F   Bb

VERSE

1. The Lord said There is no man or wo - man

Bb   Eb   Bb

That can-not find a place in His love

Eb   Bb

And there is no sin that's big-ger than His mer - cy

Dm   Ebmaj.7   Cm7

(v. 2 ♪ ♪)

So there's a place for you in heav'n a - bove.

Bb   F7   Bb   Cm7

2. Whoever hears His knock upon their heart's door
    However faint that knocking might be
    You can be sure His arms will be wide open
    And there's a place for you and a place for me.
         Chorus

290 Do you know about my Saviour

Words and Music: D. Lowe
arr. N.L. Warren

Do you know a-bout Je-sus born in sta-ble bare? Do you know a-bout Je-sus com-ing down His love to share? Do you know a-bout Je-sus or don't you real-ly care? Do you know a-bout my Lord?

Do you know about my Saviour who died on Calvary?
Do you know about my Saviour hanging there in agony?
Do you know about my Saviour who loves you and me?
Do you know about my Lord?

Now today we hear a lot about the atom bomb and things,
Have you any time to think about the peace that Jesus brings?
Do you listen to the Christian who of his Saviour sings?
Do you know about my Lord?

291 Tell me the way

Words and Music: R.T. Bewes
arr. M.C.T. Strover

We're in a great race to put rock-ets in space, But the
needs of our souls we're re - fus - ing to face; I
search my - self through for a pur-pose that's true, For

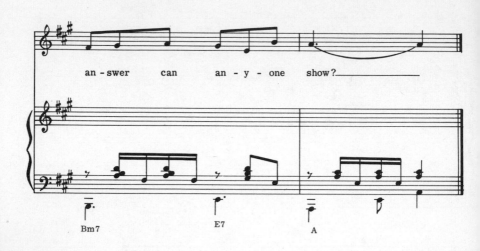

an - swer   can   an - y - one   show?

Bm7   E7   A

2.   There are Minis and Jags and plenty of fags,
     And money comes easy without many snags,
     Position to win, with a pension thrown in,
     But life is empty, and drags.
          Chorus

3.   As a kid I was given one free day in seven,
     With bangers for breakfast and church at eleven;
     Now a garden I weed, Sunday scandal I read,
     Clean car, but no thought of Heaven.
          Chorus

4.   To conform is the way in the world of today,
     A world of sick humour and moral decay;
     Love's easy and free, the experts agree,
     But life is swinging away.
          Chorus

5.   If God could just dwell on earth for a spell,
     A God who could save from the boredom of hell;
     And if pain could be shared by a Saviour who cared,
     Then why does nobody tell?
          Chorus

Songs and Spirituals

292 My soul is a witness for my Lord

Words and Music: Traditional
arr. O. J. Thomas

died and went to heaven, Lord, | in-a due time, Now Meth-us 'lah was a wit - ness
killed a-bout a thousand of | the Philistine.   O | Sam-son was a wit-ness

Bb   F9 F7 Bb   Eb   Dm   Bb

for my   Lord,   Meth -us-'lah was a wit - ness | for my   Lord. My
for my   Lord,   Samson was a wit - ness | for my   Lord. My

Gm   D7   Eb   Bb   C7   F7   Bb Cm7

Verse 3:

Now Dan - i-el was a   He -brew child,   He went to   pray to his

Eb   Bb Eb   Bb   Eb   Bb7 Eb Bb

God a - while; The king at   once for   Dan-iel did sen',   And he

Eb Bb7 Eb Bb   Gm D7 Gm   Eb   Bb C9

Softly

put him right down in the li-ons' den! God sent His an-gels the

Bb   D7   Gm   Eb   F7   Bb   Gm   D7   Gm

Slowly

li - ons for to keep, An' Dan-iel lay down an' went to sleep!

Eb   Dm   F7   Bb7   Eb   Ebm6   Bb

Now Dan-iel was a wit-ness for my Lord, now Dan-iel was a wit - ness

Eb   Bb   Gm   D7   Eb   Bb   Bbm

Refrain: after v. 3 only

for my Lord. O my soul is a wit-ness for my Lord, My

C7   F7   Bb   Bb   Eb   Bb   Eb   D7

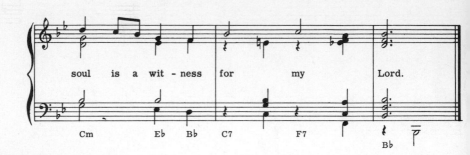

soul   is   a wit - ness   for   my   Lord.

Cm   Eb   Bb   C7   F7   Bb

293 My Lord what a morning

Words and Music: Traditional
arr.   O. J. Thomas

Slowly
Refrain:

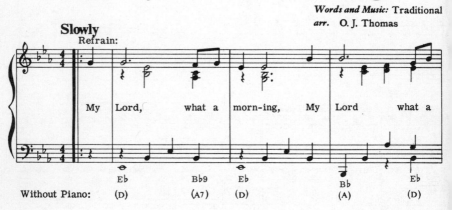

My   Lord,   what a   morn-ing, My   Lord   what a

Eb   Bb9   Eb   Bb   Eb
Without Piano: (D)   (A7)   (D)   (A)   (D)

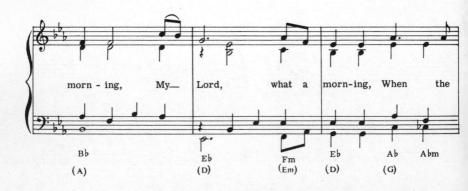

morn - ing,   My—   Lord,   what a   morn-ing, When   the

Bb   Eb   Fm   Eb   Ab   Abm
(A)   (D)   (Em)   (D)   (G)

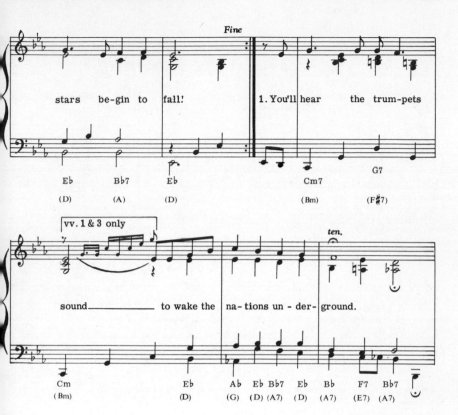

stars be-gin to fall! 1. You'll hear the trum-pets

Eb   Bb7   Eb   Cm7   G7
(D)   (A)   (D)   (Bm)   (F#7)

vv. 1 & 3 only

sound———— to wake the na-tions un-der-ground.

Cm   Eb   Ab Eb Bb7 Eb Bb   F7 Bb7
(Bm)   (D)   (G) (D)(A7)(D) (A7) (E7)(A7)

Look-ing to my Lord's right hand, When the stars be-gin to fall.

Eb7   Fm7   Eb7 Ab   Eb   Bb7   Eb
(D7)   (Em7)   (D7) (G)   (D)   (A7)   (D)

2. You'll hear the sinners moan
    To wake the nations underground
    Looking to my Lord's right hand,
    When the stars begin to fall.

3. You'll hear the Christians shout
    To wake the nations underground
    Looking to my Lord's right hand,
    When the stars begin to fall.

294　Early in the morning

Words and Music: Traditional
arr. D.G. Wilson

Well, ear-ly in the morning　　A-bout the break of

D7　　　　　　　　　　G　C6　G　　　　D7

day　　　　　I asked the Lord_____ to find the

G　C6　G　　　　　　Bm

way:____　　　　Help me find the way

Am7　　　　　D7　　　　　　　G　　C6

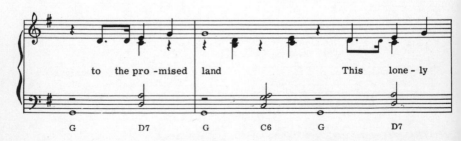

to the pro -mised land　　　　This lone - ly

G　　　D7　　G　　C6　　G　　　D7

bo- dy   needs a help - ing   hand.   I asked the

Em   A7   D7

Lord   Won't you help me   please   Help me find the

G   Bm   Am7   D7

last verse

way.

G   C6   G   C6   G   C6   G

A two-part version can be sung as follows:-   etc.

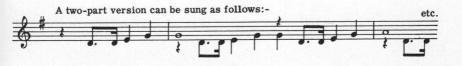

2. When the new day's a-come
    On my bed in prayer
    I pray, O Lord, won't you lead me there:
    Won't you guide me safe to the golden strand
    Won't you lead this body, this burden share?
    I asked the Lord...

3. When the judgment comes
    And the world's in chains
    And the trumpet blows, won't you call my name?
    When the thunder rolls, when the heaven's break
    And the sunshine's fire ne'er shines again,
    I asked the Lord...

295 Let my people go

Words: E.J. Bash
Tune: Traditional
arr. D.G. Wilson

Verse

O, once up-on a time a long way back, A Pha-raoh ruled, whose heart was black, And he had some slaves from the He-brew land, Who pulled the stones for the pyr - a - mids grand

Chorus:

After 1-3 And pull, you He - brews, pull,
After 4-6 O, let my peo - ple go,

Pull you He - brews,
Let my peo - ple

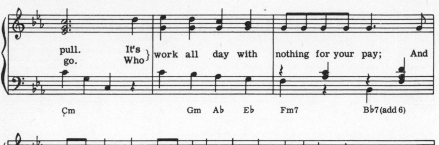

pull. It's
go. Who } work all day with nothing for your pay; And

Cm   Gm Ab Eb Fm7   Bb7 (add 6)

bur-y the lo - ser a - long the way, { And pull you He - brews
                                        O let my peo - ple

Eb   Fm9   Eb   Ab7 Bb7 Cm   Fm6   G7

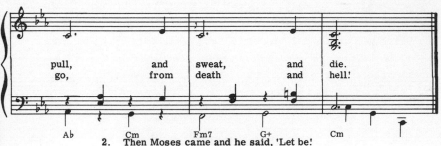

pull,   and   sweat,   and   die.
go,   from   death   and   hell!

Ab   Cm   Fm7   G+   Cm

2. Then Moses came and he said, 'Let be!
   The Hebrew people ought to be free. '
   So he killed a man to start a war,
   But the Hebrews said, 'We want no more!'
   Chorus

3. So Pharaoh called for Moses' blood
   Had Hebrews gather straw for their mud.
   And Moses fled to the wilderness,
   'I'll wash my hands of the whole blamed mess.
   Chorus

4. And God in the wilderness Moses groomed,
   Then spoke from a burning bush not consumed.
   'You go to Egypt, fear not Pharaoh,
   And tell him to let my people go. '
   Chorus

5. And Moses came with his fearful rod,
   And Egypt felt the wrath of God.
   In locusts and frogs and lice and blight,
   And first born sons dying all in the night.
   Chorus

6. Then Pharaoh rose in his grief and pain,
   And cleared the Hebrews from his domain.
   The Hebrews crossed the wild sea tame,
   And claimed their freedom in God's name.
   Chorus

296   Didn't my Lord deliver Daniel

Words and Music: Traditional
arr. O.J. Thomas

2. The wind blows east and the wind blows west,
   It blows like the Judgment Day;
   And every soul that's never prayed
   Is glad to a-pray that day!
   Didn't my Lord......

3. If the moon run down in a purple stream,
   And the sun forbear to shine,
   And the stars in the heavens all disappear,
   King Jesus shall be mine!
   Didn't my Lord......

297 I got a home in that rock

Words and Music: Traditional
arr. O.J. Thomas

heard my Sav-iour cry, "You got-ta home in-a that Rock, don't you
died he found a home on high, He had a home in-a that Rock, don't you

see.
see.

died he went to hell. He had no
wa - ter but fire next time. Bet-ter get a

Solemnly

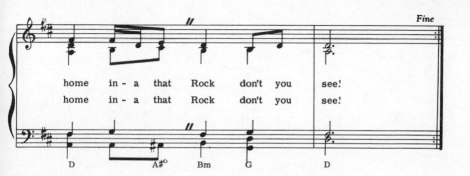

home in - a that Rock don't you see!
home in - a that Rock don't you see!

Fine

298 Come to me

Words and Music: Traditional
arr. O.J. Thomas

2. Come to Me! Jesus now gently pleads.
   Come to Me! I can supply all needs;
   And My way unto green pastures leads,
   Free from sin! Enter in! God is your home.

299 We are climbing Jacob's ladder

Words and Music: Traditional
arr. O.J. Thomas

2. Ev'ry rung goes higher 'n' higher
   Ev'ry rung goes higher 'n' higher
   Ev'ry rung goes higher 'n' higher
   Soldier of the Cross.

3. Sinner do you love my Jesus?
   Sinner do you love my Jesus?
   Sinner do you love my Jesus?
   Soldier of the Cross

4. If you love Him, why not serve Him?
   If you love Him, why not serve Him?
   If you love Him, why not serve Him?
   Soldier of the Cross.

5. Faithful prayer will make a soldier
   Faithful prayer will make a soldier
   Faithful prayer will make a soldier
   Soldier of the Cross.

6. We are climbing higher 'n' higher
   We are climbing higher 'n' higher
   We are climbing higher 'n' higher
   Soldiers of the Cross.

The first line of a piece is included, in italic type, only where it differs from the title.

FIRST PUBLISHED NOVEMBER 1969
FOURTH REPRINT 1974

Overseas Agents

EMU Book Agencies Ltd, 511 Kent Street, Sydney, NSW
Australia

CSSM and Crusader Bookroom Society Ltd, 177 Manchester Street
Christchurch, New Zealand

Sunday School Centre Wholesale, Box 3020, Cape Town
South Africa

Anglican Book Society, 228 Bank Street, Ottawa K2P IXI,
Canada

Standard Book Numbers: 85491 809 4 (Fabric)
85491 810 8 (Boards)

*Published as a Falcon Book for the Church Pastoral Aid Society,
32 Fleet Street, London EC4Y 1DB
Printed Offset Litho in Great Britain
by Cox & Wyman Ltd,
London, Fakenham and Reading*

COVER: M G O GRAPHICS